THE ONLY
Personal
Letter
Book
YOU'LL EVER NEED

Written by
Judi Barton and Nate Rosenblatt

Edited by
Carole Lefcort and Marjory Rosenblatt

Round Lake Publishing

Round Lake Publishing Co.
31 Bailey Avenue
Ridgefield, CT 06877

Printed in the United States of America

0   9   8   7   6   5   4   3   2

ISBN 0-929543-43-2

ACW-7778

Other Helpful Books from Round Lake Publishing

The following books are available from your bookseller. If they are not in stock, you may order directly from Round Lake Publishing.

Complete Book of Contemporary Business Letters
400 model letters for all areas of business, including customer relations, handling customer complaints, credit and collections, personnel relations, memos and reports, job search, personal letters and much more. 470 pages, soft cover, 6" x 8 3/4" $19.95

Encyclopedia of Money Making Sales Letters
Over 300 letters covering all phases of selling, from prospecting for new customers to closing sales. Includes responses to objections, keeping the customer buying, selling yourself, plus much more. *"Helps sell anything"*—The New York Times. 370 pages, soft cover, 6" x 8 3/4" $19.95

Step-By-Step Legal Forms and Agreements
165 legal forms for business and personal use. Includes wills, living will, power of attorney, forms for buying and selling real estate, starting a company, corporate forms, and much more. The most comprehensive book of its kind. *"Could hardly be easier to use"*—The New York Times. 440 pages, soft cover, 6" x 8 3/4" $19.95

Encyclopedia of Job-Winning Resumes
400 resumes covering every major industry and all job levels—from entry level to CEO. Also 40 cover letters for all situations, 30 resumes for difficult situations and expert advice on preparing resumes for each field. *The most comprehensive resume book ever published.* 548 pages, soft cover, 6" x 8 3/4" $16.95

Hiring, Firing (and everything in between)
160 forms covering all aspects of personnel management, including job applications, interviewing guides, personnel policies, performance appraisals, orientation, attendance, salary, discipline, benefits, termination, federal regulations, and more. 370 pages, soft cover, 6" x 8 3/4" $24.95

Order Form

Please rush me the following books:

oplb

☐ The Complete Book of Contemporary Business Letters $19.95
☐ Encyclopedia of Money Making Sales Letters $19.95
☐ Step-By-Step Legal Forms and Agreements $19.95
☐ Encyclopedia of Job-Winning Resumes $16.95
☐ Hiring, Firing (and everything in between) $24.95

Add $3.95 to the total order for shipping

I have enclosed ☐ Check   Bill my credit card   ☐ Visa   ☐ MasterCard

Credit card # _____ Exp. Date _____

Signature (required for credit card) _____

Name _____
　　　　Please print
Company _____

Address _____

City _____ State _____ Zip _____

Round Lake Publishing
31 Bailey Avenue, Ridgefield, CT 06877　　　　　　　**(203) 438-5255**

Contents

Chapter 2 COMPLAINTS

Chapter 3   CONGRATULATIONS

Congratulations on Event

Congratulations on Achievement

Saying It with a Poem

Chapter 4 CORRESPONDENCE TO FAMILY AND FRIENDS

Chapter 5   DEALING WITH BANKS, CREDIT, TAXES AND INSURANCE

Chapter 7 EXPRESSING OPINIONS

Chapter 8 GIFT CARD ONE-LINERS

Chapter 9 INTRODUCTIONS AND REFERENCES

Introductions

References

Chapter 10 INVITATIONS

Adult Invitations

Children's Invitations

Chapter 11 LETTERS TO BUILDERS AND LANDLORDS

Letters to Builders and Contractors

Chapter 12 LETTERS TO PROFESSIONALS

Chapter 13 PRAISE AND THANK YOU'S

Praise

Thank You's from Adults

Thank You's from Children

Telling It like It Is

You Hurt My Feelings

Saying No

Chapter 16 SYMPATHY AND CONDOLENCES

What this Book Will Do for You

Many of us become tongue-tied when we try to communicate our thoughts clearly. We often *mis*communicate, then wonder why we don't get the results we had hoped for.

This book takes the guesswork out of writing effective letters, and helps you take control of your life and your relationships through the written word. It contains more than 400 letters to deal with almost every situation you might encounter—from a demand for a refund on damaged goods to an apology for forgetting a loved one's birthday. You'll never again have to ask yourself, "How should I phrase this?" when you want your letter to hit the mark.

You'll learn the best ways to register a complaint, state your opinion, resolve a credit dispute or turn down an unreasonable request for a favor. Do you need a letter of recommendation? This book will show you how to ask for one, and how to write one, as well.

There are invitations for every occasion, from a class reunion to a country weekend, and thank you's for anything from flowers to financial assistance. And you'll never be at a loss for words to express sympathy or condolences.

You'll master techniques for communicating good news and bad news. And you'll learn the tactful approach for dealing with even the most difficult issues. For example, how to tell someone to stop interfering in your life, or inform your landlord that your rent check will be late.

Along with each letter, there are helpful comments to guide you in customizing your message for clarity and impact. So whether your goal is to clean up your credit rating or to tell someone to clean up their act, your written communication will be focused and effective.

How to Use This Book

The Content

Before you sit down to write, consider the purpose of your letter. Is it to cause a desired action, to explain something that requires clarification, to express a sentiment, or to get something off your chest?

Once you decide on your purpose, select the model letter in the book that comes closest to suiting your intentions. Perhaps there's a letter that fills the bill perfectly. If so, all you'll need to do is change the names on the sample and, possibly, adjust a detail or two to make it right on target.

In some cases, the letter you want may not be exactly like one in the book. But if you take a thought from one letter and combine it with a sentence or two from another, you can create just what you need. The more letters you become familiar with, the easier it will be to compose your own dynamic messages.

The introductions to each chapter will give you the fundamentals of letter writing for each category of letters, such as complaints, apologies or thank you's. The comments that accompany each letter will show you what to include and what to omit when you customize your letters. You'll find out how to write with the reader's perspective in mind, so each letter accomplishes its goal. And you'll see how a subtle change of tone or emphasis can achieve your aim.

After you finish writing a letter, read it over to be sure it's free of spelling, grammatical and factual errors and to be certain it sounds the way you intended. A good way to do this is to pretend that you're the one who is receiving the letter, and imagine how you'd react to it. If you're satisfied with the letter, go ahead and send it. If not, make any necessary changes and read it over again.

The Format

The difficult part of writing a letter is deciding what you want to say. The easy part is formatting your letter so it looks businesslike, if that's what you're trying to project, or so it looks friendly, if that's your purpose.

Letters to businesses and organizations. When you write to a business or organization, or to an individual in any context but a social one, use a business format.

For simplicity sake, and for easy readability, the letters in this book are all formatted in full block style, with a centered letterhead— a style that is attractive and professional looking. The form below shows the correct spacing for full block style:

Name
Address
City, State Zip

1 to 12 blank lines depending on length of letter (for shorter letters leave more blank lines)
Date
1 to 12 blank lines depending on length of letter (for shorter letters leave more blank lines)
Person's name
Title (If appropriate)
Company or organization
Street address
City, State Zip
double space
Dear (salutation):
double space
First paragraph, body of the letter begins. (This is always single spaced with the paragraphs starting at the left margin.)
double space
Next paragraph
double space
Last paragraph
double space
Sincerely yours,
quadruple space

(Signature)
Typed name
double space
Enclosure (if appropriate)

Social correspondence. Social letters differ substantially in format from letters you write to companies and organizations.

First of all, you needn't use a letterhead, and an inside address is not only unnecessary, but inappropriate. Your salutation (Dear Bill) should be followed by a comma, rather than a colon, indicating a more informal style, and you have wide latitude to vary from the full block style. A popular variation would be:

September 19, 19XX

Dear Joe,

    I couldn't help noticing that you seemed particularly happy when I saw you last Thursday. It's possible that your new job has you elated, but my guess is that it's more likely your recent move to a new house is causing your positive attitude.
    In any case, you have much to be thankful for. Enjoy all the good things that have come your way. Congratulations!

Love,

Betsy

    These days, most people find computer-printed or typewritten letters acceptable for almost every circumstance. But to make your social correspondence truly personal, and especially if deep emotions are involved (as in condolence letters or love letters), it should be hand written. Choose either plain or personalized social stationary or note cards that reflect your personality and the occasion.

Apologies 1

It can be embarrassing to find yourself in a situation where a written apology seems necessary. But, by making the decision to send such a letter, you're taking a giant first step toward making amends. You're presenting yourself as someone who's mature enough to take responsibility for their own behavior.

Before beginning your letter, focus on what you want to accomplish. Are you apologizing because you're genuinely remorseful for something, or is it just a courtesy? There's a big difference between a polite apology to excuse your absence from a social event and an apology where the words will salvage a damaged relationship. Remember, in either case, your objective is to appease the reader—not to make a bad situation worse.

Keep the reader's feelings in mind as you write your apology, and express the degree of remorse or regret that matches the circumstances. If your beloved Great Dane relieved himself on a friend's priceless Persian carpet, it's appropriate for you to offer to pay to have the carpet cleaned. It isn't necessary for you to offer to put Rover to sleep.

On the other hand, if you've forgotten a loved one's birthday or anniversary, your letter had better put your heart on your sleeve. Leave no question in the reader's mind about just how devastated you feel about your blunder.

Apologies about events. When you're apologizing for events, keep the following objectives in mind:

1. Admit that you misbehaved, missed the event, or missed the point.
2. Express your regret.
3. Indicate that you plan to take action to make amends. (Offer to pay for damages, promise to change your behavior, etc.) Be sure to follow up, or you'll risk losing your credibility.

If there were extenuating circumstances, it's okay to mention them. But remember—the key ingredient in a sincere apology is *accepting* blame, not *dodging* it.

Apologies about feelings. So you've hurt someone's feelings. You've said something insensitive, or you've betrayed a confidence. Feelings are uniquely personal. What seems like an off-handed remark to you, may be an insult to someone else. That's why writing an apology about feelings requires a tactful approach.

Begin with the premise that the reader is entitled to their feelings, and that you respect those feelings. By doing so, you're avoiding conflict, and making the reader more receptive to your apology. Emphasize how much you value the relationship, ask for forgiveness, and promise not to repeat the offending behavior.

Name
Address
City, State Zip

Date

Dear Polly,

I'm not sure which was worse: my lack of judgment in bringing Andy to your luncheon, or my inability to control him. He's at a stage where he can't be exposed to polite company... which, of course, you observed first-hand.

When my babysitter cancelled at the last minute, I should have swallowed my disappointment, called, and told you I couldn't make it. But I wanted to see you and the rest of the gang so badly that I acted without thinking of anyone but myself.

Rather than recount everything Andy (and I) did to help ruin the afternoon, I'll offer a blanket apology. His behavior was more hyper than usual, and I wish I had shown more sense than to bring him.

I'm sorry, Polly. Take as long as you need to forgive me, but please forgive me.

Your repentant friend,

Elaine

- Apologize in terms that show that you are sincerely sorry.

- Acknowledge the poor behavior, but don't irritate the reader further by listing all the misdeeds.

Name
Address
City, State Zip

Date

Dear Rocco,

When I erected a fence between your property and mine, I assumed that it would end my dog's raids on your yard. I obviously underestimated his digging skills.

I've repaired the fence and added mesh that should end Lucky's unwelcome visits. And, of course I'll pay for replacing the shrubs he destroyed.

I really appreciate your not making a big issue of this. In a sense, you've gotten some revenge for this incident because the plants he ate didn't agree with Lucky. We had quite a clean-up last night!

Thanks for being such a great neighbor. I apologize for the inconvenience.

Cordially,

Bart

- Don't rationalize your pet's bad behavior; apologize for it.

- Describe what you're doing to correct the offensive behavior.

Name
Address
City, State Zip

Date

Dear Anne,

The more your guests laughed, the more I clowned around. It never occurred to me that I was having more fun at your party than you were.

As you know, I've always loved having an audience. But my "performance" was at your expense. I was ungracious and totally out of order, and I apologize.

It was such a lovely party, except for my antics. I'm sorry I upset you. Please forgive me.

Regretfully,

Sandy

• No matter how unintentional your poor behavior might have been, accept responsibility for your lack of judgement.

• Even if you said you were sorry in person, a follow-up letter shows you continued to feel remorse.

Name
Address
City, State Zip

Date

Mr. Lee Forester
James & Foster, Inc.
One Meridian Plaza
Chicago, IL 60606

Dear Lee:

I was really looking forward to attending your company's Wallace A. Buchanan Lifetime Achievement Award presentation—particularly since you were the recipient—but mother nature hissed at me.

I had to wrap up a trip in Indianapolis that day, and I thought if I left by 3:00 o'clock, I'd easily be back in time. As you probably know, a snow and ice storm hit the area, and that 180 mile drive might as well have been 1,800 miles. I didn't even reach the state line.

While I'm disappointed I wasn't able to attend, I'm very pleased that you invited me to share your special evening. Congratulations on a well-earned, richly-deserved award.

Cordially,

Henry Dale

- Don't go too deeply into details about the circumstances of missing the event (the reader may find them less than compelling!).

- Show that you, too, are disappointed.

Name
Address
City, State Zip

Date

Dear Jon and Evelyn,

The enclosed check speaks for itself. It will cover the cost of purchasing the same kind of CD player that slipped through my fingers during your party. The apology requires some explaining.

I had never seen a unit quite like yours, and you know how I am about electronic gadgets. I can't resist an up-close-and-personal inspection. I don't know why it fell, but fall it did.

I'm really sorry. Will you give me a chance to be more careful next time? Please call to let me know I've been forgiven.

Your clumsy friend,

Ted

- If you break something of value, covering the cost of repair or replacement makes an apology palatable.

- You can be as innovative with your sign-off as the situation demands. "Sincerely," "Yours very truly," and the like are more formal and not mandatory among friends.

Name
Address
City, State Zip

Date

Dear Rose,

If you noticed that I skulked out of your house Saturday night, it was because I was so embarrassed I couldn't look you in the eye. I'm the one who burned the hole in your new sofa. I was so mortified, my first reaction was to run.

Please allow me to pay for the repair. I'd be happy to make arrangements with an upholsterer I've worked with to have the sofa picked up at your convenience. I'll call in a few days to find out what's best for you.

Aside from my blunder, it was one great party! Thanks for inviting me. I hope you'll forgive me for the accident and the unconscionable way I dealt with it.

Sincerest regrets,

Alice

- Explain what happened, and how you feel about it. Don't trivialize the incident.

- Offer to take care of any expense, and be sure to follow up in good faith.

Name
Address
City, State Zip

Date

Dear Jim,

Even though I can't seem to remember how I acted last Saturday, enough people have made it a point to tell me, which somehow makes me feel doubly embarrassed.

I'm sorry for the verbal abuse I threw at you for taking my car keys away. You obviously did me a giant favor, and I repaid you with insults. You're a remarkable person to have taken a stand, particularly when it would have been far easier to just turn your back on me.

I'm sorry I let myself get into that state, and I'm particularly sorry that I made things so difficult for you. I won't let it happen again.

Thanks for caring enough to put up with me. You're a great friend.

Gratefully,

Lou

- Acknowledge your behavior.

- While an apology may be good enough, a promise never to repeat the behavior is even better.

Sorry I Can't Come to Your Party (1-08)

Name
Address
City, State Zip

Date

Dear Lorraine and Tom,

Did you ever wish you could be in two places at once? I'm feeling that way about the upcoming weekend. Your anniversary bash sounds like the event of the year. But the timing is bad for us. Our niece is making her First Communion in Atlanta and, as her godparents, Bill and I are committed to being there.

We're disappointed that we'll miss celebrating your twenty-five years of togetherness.

We'd like to toast you belatedly when we return. How about dinner at Smokey's? I'll call you to set a date. Meanwhile, congratulations!

Best always,

Miriam

- Let the reader know that you appreciate and understand the importance of the occasion.

- If you value the friendship, be specific about why you can't attend, and suggest a future get-together.

Name
Address
City State Zip

Date

Dear Penny,

Some friend I am! Would it help if I said I forgot your birthday because I think of you as ageless?

If flattery won't earn your forgiveness, how about letting me take you to lunch at Chez Nous next Friday? Champagne and the works?

I'll call Monday to confirm.

Your chagrined pal,

Doris

- A little self-deprecation doesn't hurt if you've overlooked an occasion.

- Let the reader know your apology is sincere, and prove it by offering to make it up in some tangible way.

Name
Address
City, State Zip

Date

Dear Lisa,

Somebody you know is a dope,
A husband who's quite without hope.
Your birthday's forgotten,
He's feeling so rotten
He doesn't know quite how to cope.

If he just could get back in your graces,
He would take you to fabulous places.
Let him make up to you,
(Which he's sure you would do,
If you just could see how red his face is!)

I love you. Will you forgive me?

Sheepishly,

Dale

• You can ease the sting of being forgetful with an admission of guilt, albeit a humorous one.

• A promise to make it up to the person may soften any hurt feelings.

Name
Address
City, State Zip

Date

Dear Nan,

Someone once asked Albert Einstein's wife if she understood the theory of relativity. She said, "No, but I understand Dr. Einstein."

Well, you might not understand how I could forget our anniversary, but you do understand me well enough to know that I'll try very hard to make my blunder up to you. In fact, when I get home from this interminable trip, I'm planning a special evening for us at Le Champignon and a surprise I'm sure will please you.

Please forgive me, sweetheart. I may have missed our anniversary date, but I treasure every day that we've been married. I love you very much.

Your devoted (but forgetful) husband,

Michael

• There's no sense making excuses for forgetting an occasion that's this important. If you blew it, just admit it and go on from there.

• A bit of suspense can be disarming and diverting. A little romance can salve hurt feelings.

Name
Address
City, State Zip

Date

Dear Molly,

I'm so embarrassed. I blamed you for spreading a rumor about me, and I just discovered you had nothing to do with it.

I feel foolish for jumping to a conclusion without knowing all the facts. My anger was totally misplaced.

There aren't enough words to tell you how much I value your friendship. I can't forgive myself, but can you forgive me?

With love,

Arnetta

- Accept the blame and ask for forgiveness.

- The details of the error aren't as important as the sincerity of your apology.

Name
Address
City, State Zip

Date

Dear Marsha,

Trust is an important part of friendship. I think of myself as a good friend and that's why I would never betray your trust without a valid reason.

I discussed your personal affairs with Mike in an effort to bring you two back together. I felt that our mutual concern for you justified my confiding in him. Now I realize that, however noble my intentions, I was wrong to intercede without your permission.

Will you forgive me? Please!

Your friend,

Babette

- Admit that you were wrong.

- Offer an explanation (not an excuse).

Name
Address
City, State Zip

Date

Dear Sharon,

My intentions are usually good, but the execution is, on occasion, lacking. I don't always think about the consequences of my words, but you've made it clear that I will have to, if our relationship is to continue.

I love you very much, and I'm sorry I hurt you. I'm glad you care enough about us to let me know when I've stepped over the line.

Please forgive me,

Edward

- Make it clear that you take responsibility for the hurt.

- Ask for forgiveness. The request demonstrates you are not taking the relationship for granted.

Name
Address
City, State Zip

Date

Dear Betsy,

I've compounded an error and made a bigger fool of myself than even I thought possible.

First, in order to avoid you, I lied and told you I would be away for the weekend. My feelings were hurt when you won the ESTEEM account and I didn't. False pride kept me from telling you I was resentful, and I needed time to get over it.

Then, when we ran into each other at the movies, I was so embarrassed I couldn't speak; that's why I walked right past you. I've dug a hole for myself, and now I'm trying to climb out of it.

I value you as a friend and as a colleague. Please accept my apology for my childish behavior. It's time I grew up and dealt with my feelings more maturely.

Most sincerely,

Constance

- Tell the truth, accept the blame, then apologize.

- Explain why you want to set things right.

Name
Address
City, State Zip

Date

Dear Rick,

I feel I can discuss almost anything with you. In fact, I feel more comfortable with you than with many of my women friends. Lately, though, I've sensed some tension when we're together, and I think I'm to blame.

I'm afraid my warm feelings toward you have been misinterpreted, and you've begun to think I'm looking for something more than friendship. I'm not; and I'm sorry if I gave you the wrong impression.

I hope our relationship can weather this misunderstanding. I don't want to lose a good friend and confidant.

Always,

Inez

• Tell the reader what you value about the relationship.

• Define your view of the relationship.

Name
Address
City, State Zip

Date

Dear Wayne,

I guess I've been reading too many romance novels. It didn't occur to me that a man could invite me to his hotel room without seduction in mind. I overreacted and I'm sorry.

I really <u>would</u> love to see the video of your lecture. Will you invite me again?

Cordially,

Sylvia

- Explain how the misunderstanding occurred.

- Tell the reader how you'd like to make amends.

Name
Address
City, State Zip

Date

Dear Lloyd,

My timing was off yesterday. I pressed you for a decision about our vacation plans without knowing that you'd just been notified of your Dad's illness. I understand why you were upset, and I'm sorry.

I'd like to be more sensitive to your feelings, but I need your help. If something is bothering you, please tell me. It's frustrating trying to read your mind.

At this moment, your father's health is our priority. Let's talk about how we can support him through this episode.

Love,

Diana

- If you're at fault admit it.

- Make a suggestion about how to avoid future arguments.

Name
Address
City, State Zip

Date

Dear Bruce,

I'm sorry I jumped down your throat during our card game...
particularly since I've discovered that I didn't know what I was
talking about.

You had the facts right, and I had 'em wrong. You acted like a
gentleman, and I acted like an idiot. Even if I had been right, I
would still have been out of line.

I apologize. If you're willing to forgive my tantrum, I'll give you my
word that I won't subject you to that kind of adolescent display
again.

My apologies,

Kevin

- There's no easier way to diffuse a bad situation than to say "I'm sorry, I was wrong, and it won't happen again."

- In an informal letter, stylistic adaptations (e.g., using "'em" instead of "them") are acceptable.

Name
Address
City, State Zip

Date

Dear Wendy,

When I saw you in the Commerce building lobby the other day, you were deep in conversation with a group of people. Even though I wanted to say hello, I decided not to intrude on what appeared to be an intense discussion.

Not only was there no slight intended, I'm disappointed that you'd think I would intentionally ignore you. I had no way of knowing your conversation was social and open to an "outsider."

Anyway, let's forget it, shall we? I think our friendship can withstand this misunderstanding.

Fondly,

Margaret

- Don't apologize for something you didn't do; it makes you seem guilty.

- You can turn the situation around so that the reader has to take responsibility for the misunderstanding.

Complaints 2

There's one in every crowd: the whiner. The person who complains about virtually everything. Unfortunately, complaining is rarely a prelude to action—it's an end in itself.

The person who takes the time to write a complaint letter, however, *is* action-oriented. That's the purpose of a complaint letter: to bring about a change in policy or behavior or to establish legitimate grounds for restitution.

Complaints to neighbors. A great deal of tact is required when writing a complaint letter to a neighbor. After all, you're going to have to face this person each day when you step outside to retrieve the morning paper or empty the trash.

If your neighbor is neglecting their property, begin your letter by invoking a sense of community pride. Impress upon them how hard you (and the other neighbors) work to keep your street looking its best. Mention the effect of an ill-kempt yard on real estate values. Then tell the reader what action you want taken.

If you want your neighbor to *cease* an action, describe how that activity affects you, your children, or your property. Offer a suggested remedy or two. Express your hope that the issue can be settled amicably—without taking legal steps. Try to end the letter on a cordial, "neighborly" note.

Complaints to companies about employees. Decide before you write this kind of letter exactly what action you're seeking. Do you want the person fired, or simply reprimanded? Unless the offense was egregious, (such as reckless driving by a trucker), you might not think it's worth having some poor fellow's pink slip on your conscience. Describe exactly what happened (who, what, when, where and how); then suggest to the reader what action you think is appropriate. A subtle reminder about personal grooming? A mandatory course in customer relations? Reparations for your damaged garage door? Think about what your demands are, then state them *firmly*.

Complaints to companies about products and services. These are straightforward, no-frills demands for restitution. You need to provide a detailed account of the facts and circumstances surrounding your complaint, and furnish documentation to back it up. Establish a reasonable deadline for response, and state your intention to work your way up the chain of command until your demands are met.

Name
Address
City, State Zip

Date

Dear Lew,

If you were sitting in my living room, looking across the street at your home, here's what you'd see: a rusted water heater, a chipped, discolored bathtub, three out-of-commisssion lawn-mowers, a bunch of broken screens and other unsightly items in your driveway.

I've waited over a year to ask you to move the material, because I just kept assuming you'd get around to it. By now, it may have reached the point where you're so used to it, you don't even see it. (I know that's happened to me: Until Julie told me that the paint on our house was cracked and peeling, I never noticed it.)

Please move the material out of sight or simply put it out with the trash. If you need help moving any of those items, my son and I would be glad to lend a hand.

Thanks for the consideration.

Sincerely,

Tony

• Try to make the reader see the situation as you see it, without attacking their integrity.

• An offer to help expresses willingness to cooperate with the reader.

Name
Address
City, State Zip

Date

Dear Mr. Sloane,

I feel fortunate to live in a beautiful neighborhood like ours. That's probably why I take such pride in maintaining the appearance of my property. I wouldn't want real estate values to decline for <u>anyone</u> in Crestwood!

It concerns me that your lawn has gone unmown for weeks now, which diminishes the appearance of the entire street. If there is some reason why you have been unable to care for your property, I know the neighbors would be happy to pitch in to help.

Otherwise, everyone on Maple Grove Road would appreciate it if you would return to mowing your lawn regularly, as you always have in the past.

Thanks.

Sincerely,

Russell Osterwald

• Explain that one overgrown lawn brings the entire street down a notch.

• Offer to help out if the homeowner is temporarily unable to care for their property.

Name
Address
City, State Zip

Date

Dear Joanna,

One of the joys of having a pool is being able to share it with friends. But along with pool ownership comes responsibility for the safety of everyone who uses it. In fact, the township requires us to have a fence around the pool area to discourage unauthorized swimming.

Twice this past week I came home from work and found Matt and Troy in the pool. There were no adults around.

Joanna, as I've offered in the past, anytime you or your boys want to swim, call me. If it's convenient, I'll tell you so. But for everyone's safety, be sure that the boys never use the pool without permission and supervision.

Thanks.

Cordially,

Ava

- Let the reader know that you're not inhospitable; there's a safety issue involved.

- Be specific about your rules and stick to them.

Name
Address
City, State Zip

Date

Dear Mr. Hoyt,

Your new fence looks great. I wish I could say the same for my garden. Your workers trampled the flowers I recently planted: six flats of impatiens, a dozen geraniums, and a dozen pansies.

I put a lot of effort and expense into my garden. I'm willing to do the replanting, but I'd like to be reimbursed for the cost of new plants, which was $63.

I'll call you at the end of the week to arrange for the payment.

Thanks.

Cordially,

Maryellen Arzt

• Make it clear that you expect to be repaid.

• Say when you intend to follow up.

Name
Address
City, State Zip

Date

Dear Howard,

I'm pleased to hear how well your deck turned out. I'm sorry I couldn't give you more of a hand, but at least my tools were there to represent me.

Now I need to get started on a few projects of my own by the end of this month...but I'm short on tools at the moment! Maybe we can kill two birds with one stone: Why don't you and Ellen plan to spend a day with us soon, and bring the tools along with you?

Call me or Mary Beth so we can make a date. We're looking forward to seeing you again. Maybe you can give me a few tips on remodeling my kitchen.

Cordially,

Steve

- Asking for something to be returned doesn't have to be confrontational or embarrassing.

- Even though the letter is friendly, make it clear that it's the reader's responsibility to return the tools.

Name
Address
City, State Zip

Date

Dear Sam,

One of the things I like about our neighborhood is that people help each other. I was happy to lend you my lawnmower, because I felt confident it would be well cared for.

Unfortunately, since you used the lawnmower, I haven't been able to start it and one of the blades is bent. I had the mower serviced at the beginning of the season and had only used it once, so I know it was in good condition when you borrowed it.

I'm taking the mower to Howell's Lawn and Garden Center to be checked. I hope I can count on you to pay for the repair. When I have an estimate, I'll stop by.

Sam, let's not allow this mishap to interfere with the great relationship we've enjoyed these past years.

Cordially,

Joe Burgmayer

• Keep the tone cordial, but be clear about your expectations for the repair.

• Let the reader know you hope one incident won't spoil the friendship.

Name
Address
City, State Zip

Date

Dear Mr. McConaghy,

I'm a nurse who works long and hard hours. A good night's sleep is critical to my performance on the job.

For the past week, your dog has made it impossible for me to get any rest. He starts barking just as I'm trying to go to sleep, and he continues non-stop into the early morning.

The loss of sleep is starting to affect my work and I can't allow that to happen. Please find a way to keep your dog quiet.

Thank you.

Sincerely,

Maxine Greaves, R.N.

• Explain any special circumstances that might gain the reader's cooperation.

• Be cordial, but make your point.

Name
Address
City, State Zip

Date

Dear Peg,

I've always enjoyed the sounds of happiness that come from your back yard. I really think you're the best hostess in the world. Where you get the energy to entertain nearly every weekend is beyond me; I seem to need my weekends just to recuperate so I can go back to work on Monday!

I'd appreciate a favor. Would you please keep an eye on where your guests park? I'm reluctant to interrupt your get-togethers to ask people to move their cars so they don't block my driveway. But it's becoming more than an occasional nuisance.

Thanks so much.

Cordially,

Bryna Smith

• Starting your letter with a compliment can ease the sting of a complaint.

• Even though you're clearly in the right, you can maintain a relationship by asking for help rather than demanding a correction.

Name
Address
City, State Zip

Date

Dear Mrs. Metzger,

For the past week my son, Billy, has been arriving home from school in tears. Yesterday he confessed to me that your son has been forcing him to turn over his lunch money every day this week. Peter threatened Billy with a beating if he told anyone what was going on.

Billy is seven years old. Peter is eleven. Naturally, Billy is intimidated by an older, bigger boy who is making threats.

I haven't reported these events to the school authorities because I wanted to give you the opportunity to deal with the problem privately with your son. However, if the behavior doesn't change immediately, I'll notify the school authorities and follow up with them until the matter is resolved.

Sincerely,

Roxanne Thaler

- Describe the behavior that has prompted you to write the letter.

- Notify the reader that if the offensive behavior doesn't stop, you'll take the problem to a higher authority.

Name
Address
City, State Zip

Date

Dear Marla,

If my son or daughter had taken something without asking permission, I'd want to know about it. Knowing you as well as I do, I'm confident you feel the same way. Which brings me to the reason for this note.

When Richie stayed with us last weekend, he fell in love with Jesse's baseball card collection, particularly his Mike Schmidt rookie card. Richie kept putting the card in his shirt pocket, and Jesse kept reminding him to take it out.

Just before you picked Richie up Sunday evening, the card was missing again. Jesse insisted that Richie had it, but Richie denied it. I would have said something to you that evening, but I wanted to search through Jesse's room first.

Since the boys played with the cards only in Jesse's room, and since no one else was in the room that weekend, I'm asking if you would check with Richie. Jesse's so upset his card is missing (and so's his dad, who says the card is valuable).

Thanks for helping. I'll call you in a few days to see if Richie was able to shed some light on the disappearance.

Sincerely yours,

Laura

• There's no easy way to suggest to a parent that their child took something. Asking for help in resolving the situation is better than making outright accusations.

• Remember that you're dealing with both parents' and children's feelings.

Name
Address
City, State Zip

Date

Ms. Elaine Branch
Personnel Manager
Jiffy Supermarket
Garden Grove Road
Montpelier, VT 05602

Dear Ms. Branch:

I'm annoyed at myself for not having the presence of mind to respond immediately to an ethnic slur made by one of your cashiers. The comment wasn't directed at me, but that didn't make it any less offensive.

As I walked past a checkout counter, I overheard one of your clerks telling a joke to another clerk. It didn't seem to matter to her that she told the joke loudly enough to attract attention, or that what she was saying was racist. In fact, she was so open about it, she may not have been aware of how insensitive her words were.

Rather than asking you to single out the young woman, I'd like your assurance that the store will review and enforce sensitivity training with your employees. And I'll give you my assurance that if I ever hear another racial comment in your store, (a) you'll lose a good customer, and (b) I'll register a complaint with the president of your company.

I look forward to hearing from you.

Sincerely,

Wayne Solomon

- A "cool" letter can be very effective with a hot issue. This is far more effective than demanding termination or discipline.

- If you want a response, ask for it.

Name
Address
City, State Zip

Date

Mr. Nathaniel Stavros
The Windsor Cafe
1000 Newport Road
Potomac, MD 20854

Dear Mr. Stavros:

I think the food in your restaurant is wonderful, but I may never have the chance to enjoy it again. At least not until one of your waiters (his name tag read "GIANNI") either leaves or is taught how to deal with women customers.

During lunch, your waiter felt free to comment on my figure and my clothes. And he topped it off by noting that I also needed to smile more, intimating that he might be of help in that regard.

I suspect you've lost more than a few customers due to this obnoxious employee. If you don't want to lose more, I strongly suggest you do something about his behavior.

Sincerely,

Barri Thomas

• The threat of losing business guarantees that your letter will be read by management.

• Detail what you considered offensive; otherwise the behavior can't be corrected.

Your Salesperson Has an Offensive Odor (2-13)

Name
Address
City, State Zip

Date

Mr. Charles Allen
Allen Appliances
440 Harvey Road
Albuquerque, NM 87107

Dear Mr. Allen:

I visited your store near closing time on Tuesday, and approached a salesperson to ask some questions. But I was so repelled by the odor of cigar smoke, both from his breath and his clothing, that all I could think of was getting away from him. I mumbled that I was late for an appointment and left.

The next day, motivated by the good things I had heard about your pricing and service, I decided to make a return visit, this time in the morning. I didn't give it a second thought when the same salesperson smiled and started to walk towards me. Unfortunately, the odor was just as bad.

I didn't even make an excuse this time; I just spun around and left. I can't help but wonder how often this scene is repeated in your store. And I also wonder if the people who work there have a sense of smell. How can you stand it?

I don't know the salesperson's name, but you shouldn't have any trouble knowing who I'm talking about. You owe it to your customers—and this oblivious man—to do something about it.

Sincerely,

Grace Boyle

- People cannot correct problems if they're not aware of them.

- Any respectable business owner would want to be informed that sales are being lost due to a correctable problem.

Name
Address
City, State Zip

Date

General Manager
Hardison's Apparel
Blossom Drive
Charleston, SC 29412

Dear Sir or Madam:

One of your saleswomen offended me, and unless she's reprimanded and retrained, I won't be returning to your store. Her name is Clarice.

I was trying on bathing suits (as if that isn't traumatic enough!), and had narrowed my selections down to four. I asked Clarice which two she thought looked best. Her response was, "If you don't lose fifteen pounds, it doesn't matter which one you buy."

Obviously, she doesn't work on commission, but that's no excuse for her rudeness and insensitivity. I got dressed immediately and left the store without making a purchase.

If you expect to stay in business, you'd better pay more attention to your employees' attitudes. Please let me know how you plan to correct this problem.

Sincerely,

Charlene Perkins

- Describe the offending salesperson's behavior.

- State your expectation of a response.

Name
Address
City, State Zip

Date

Mr. Robert Luongo, Manager
Chez Pierre
6400 Western Boulevard
West Valley City, UT 84119

Dear Mr. Luongo:

Last Friday evening, the coat I wore to your restaurant disap-
peared from your cloakroom while I was dining. It was bad
enough that your cloak room attendant allowed my coat to "walk,"
but her complete indifference to the loss made it even more
infuriating.

You can either (1) Produce the coat within a week (full-length
leather, black, size medium, fleece-lined, with a Calla Newell
label), or (2) send me a check for $425 to cover a replacement.
And speaking of a replacement, you might consider hiring a new
cloak room attendant who takes her responsibilities more seriously.

I'll expect to hear from you by October 2nd.

Sincerely,

Barbara Banks

- Describe what was lost.

- Specify what action you expect and when.

Name
Address
City, State Zip

Date

Mr. Desmond Wilson
Andrews Appliances
322 Ligonier Road
Bloomington, MN 55420

Dear Mr. Wilson:

Despite your assurances that it wouldn't happen, your deliverymen scratched my new hardwood floor when they delivered my refrigerator.

What makes this particularly galling is that we discussed the sequence of events beforehand. You strongly urged me to have the flooring put down before the delivery. You said it would be easier for the flooring people, and that there would be less wear and tear on the refrigerator if it didn't need to be lifted to install the new floor. As things turned out, it was easier on everyone but me.

The flooring company—at a cost of $375—will sand the floor and refinish it. Since your deliverymen caused the damage, and since you guaranteed that the delivery would be damage-free, I expect you to pay for it.

You can either mail the check to me this week, or I can pick it up on the way home from work. I'll call to confirm arrangements.

Sincerely,

Margo Lender

- There's plenty of time to negotiate later, if necessary. Take a strong stand and demand full payment to start with.

- Be very clear as to whatever action you want taken (e.g., check sent, telephone response, etc.).

Name
Address
City, State Zip

Date

Mr. John Majors
Majors Auto Repair
208 State Highway
Lafayette, IN 47901

Dear Mr. Majors:

I may not be an expert in car repairs, but I know when I'm being ripped off.

I brought my 19XX LeBaron to your shop for repairs on October 23. Your mechanic, Steve, informed me that I needed a complete set of brakes. In fact, he stated that I risked an accident if I didn't have the work done immediately. After getting Steve's estimate (which was very high), I took the car to another repair shop for a second estimate.

I was informed that my brakes were in excellent condition and would require only a minor adjustment.

Because the two shops gave me such different diagnoses, I went to a third repair shop. They agreed totally with the second shop's opinion.

Your operation appears to be dishonest. I'm reporting Majors Auto Repair to The Better Business Bureau and the state consumer protection agency.

Sincerely,

Stacy Rowan

- Give an account of your experience, stating why you believe you were ripped off.

- Inform the reader that you plan to report his business to the appropriate "watchdog" agencies.

Name
Address
City, State Zip

Date

Mr. Arnold Slawek
President
Northeast Distributors
113 Canal Street
Newark, NJ 07105

Dear Mr. Slawek:

One of your truckers is driving recklessly and needs to be disciplined or dismissed.

This morning, at about 9:00, I was heading south on the Garden State Parkway near Rahway. I was traveling at the speed limit in the passing lane, when I saw a huge truck bearing down on me. As soon as it was safe, I signaled and moved to the right lane. The truck followed me there, again bearing down inches from my bumper. I moved back to the other lane and it followed. This dangerous cat and mouse game continued until I pulled off the parkway to escape. By this time I was shaking visibly.

The lettering on the truck said Northeast Distributors; the I.D. number was 84224NE. I was unable to get the entire license number, but the first three digits on the New Jersey plate were 893.

This driver is a menace. I'd like to know what you plan to do about him before I decide whether to take further action.

Very truly yours,

Margaret Nyborg

• Go right to the top with serious complaints. You're more likely to get quick action.

• Give all the details necessary to identify the vehicle.

Name
Address
City, State Zip

Date

Paoli Audio and Video
Paoli Center
Grand Rapids, MI 49508

Dear Sir or Madam:

Last month I purchased the Misumi Audio Component System
MSM-3220 from your Christmas catalog. The system is defective,
and I want to exchange it for a new unit. All my CD's jump during
play, regardless of how I position the unit.

Here's the information you need to process my exchange:

Date of Purchase: December 4,19XX
Method of Payment: Check #195, issued by Firstbank
Amount of check: $821.59

Please notify me when I can expect delivery of the new system
and when the defective unit will be picked up.

Thank you.

Very truly yours,

Wendall Lapham

• Identify the product and explain the defect.

• Give details of the purchase (e.g., date, method of payment, amount,etc.).

Name
Address
City, State Zip

Date

Handyman Helpmates, Inc.
P.O. Box 2098
San Jose, CA 95113

   Re: Deckmate Picnic Partner
        Item No.: 1PP 23970
        Price: $189.50
        Date of Purchase: April 2,19XX
        Method of payment: Check #1209 Gibralter Savings

Dear Sir or Madam:

Trying to assemble your "Deckmate Picnic Partner" table and benches almost caused a divorce in my family. Finally, my husband and I realized that we weren't inadequate; your directions were.

I thought the problems had ended when we put all the pieces together, but that's when your product's poor design became apparent. The benches fit so close to the table that we could barely squeeze into the seats (we're of average weight).

Your product is impossible to use. I want to return the unit for a full refund, as guaranteed in your catalog.

I await a check in the amount of $189.50 and instructions as to the disposal of "Deckmate Picnic Partner."

Very truly yours,

Mrs. Norman Nycz

- If you feel ripped off, say so.

- Let the reader know that your demand for a refund is non-negotiable.

Name
Address
City, State Zip

Date

Customer Service Dept.
Miracle Whiz Carpet Cleaner
822 W. Whitman Boulevard
Medford, OR 97504   Re: Money-Back Guarantee

Dear Sir or Madam:

I purchased your product based on a television advertisement that guaranteed satisfaction in the elimination of blood, pet and virtually any other kind of hard-to-remove stains from carpets. The ad claimed that Miracle Whiz Carpet Cleaner is used by hotels, theaters, offices and other high-traffic centers.

Those facilities must be satisfied to have unsightly stains on their carpets. I used your product—as directed—and found that it did nothing whatsoever. The stains just sat there. About the only positive thing I can say about Miracle Whiz is that it didn't damage my carpeting. I don't understand how you can make such outrageous claims about such an ineffective product.

I should probably complain to the FTC, but I'll settle for a prompt refund.

Sincerely,

Adam Katz

- Address your letter to Customer Service. You may find they are willing to give you more than you ask for, just to generate good will for the company.

- A mention of the FTC (Federal Trade Commission) may also help expedite your refund.

Name
Address
City, State Zip

Date

Sean Elliot
President
Hartman's Department Store
1223 Pennwood Avenue
Riverlea, OH 43085

Dear Mr. Elliot:

Early this summer, I purchased patio furniture from you. One week later, you ran an ad offering a 10% discount on all furniture. Since your advertised policy is to honor the reduced price on any merchandise purchased within 14 days of a sale, I brought my receipt to your service desk and was told the discount didn't apply to seasonal furniture.

Last week, I purchased bath towels, and then received a flyer that advertised 25% off on towels. When I tried to get the discount, I was told I had purchased towels that had already been marked down...that they were not eligible for the sale pricing. Your company always seems to have an excuse for not honoring its stated discounts.

Since I'd rather get the discount than file a complaint with the State Attorney General, I'll forego any action if you agree to honor your own policy. I've attached both sales receipts. I'll expect a positive response from you by Friday, September 12, or I'll take appropriate action.

Sincerely,

Randy Shomstein

• State the policy in question and the violation.

• Be certain the reader understands the consequences of their failure to take action.

Name
Address
City, State Zip

Date

Service Manager
Jason Electric
110 Sycamore Street
Queens Village, NY 11427

Dear Sir or Madam:

First, the good news: Your serviceperson was prompt, pleasant and courteous. He actually removed his work shoes (his idea) because he had to walk across brand new carpeting to get to the kitchen.

Now, the bad news: My oven still doesn't work properly. Your serviceperson indicated he wasn't familiar with my particular model, which makes me wonder why he was sent out on my job.

I'd appreciate it if you would send a repair person who can perform the service required. I need my oven fixed before the holidays, and I need you to live up to your reputation for fast, efficient service.

Please call me at (718) 555-0388 to schedule a new appointment.

Very truly yours,

Christa Wollenz

- You can express annoyance without tearing someone's head off.

- Tell the company what action you want taken; don't expect them to do what you want without their being told.

Name
Address
City, State Zip

Date

Mr. Warren Evans
Discount Appliances, Inc.
82 North Waverly Street
Boise, ID 83722

Dear Mr. Evans:

Have you ever noticed how television news loves to play up
"Business Bilks Customer" stories? How the owners always come
off as Scrooges and scoundrels? How businesses immediately
sag when the stories air?

Well, brace yourself, Mr. Evans, because it's about to happen to
you. Picture yourself as the feature story on the news this
Thursday, as the local consumer reporter barges into your store
demanding to know why you won't honor the warranty for a
refrigerator purchased by a struggling single mother.

If you don't like the picture, I suggest you have a repairman here
by Wednesday, June 12. I'm angry that your continual lies and
broken promises have forced me to resort to this sort of action. I'll
do whatever it takes to get you to fulfill your obligation to me.

Sincerely,

Kristin Jurgens

- Letters with time limits should be sent via a method that provides proof of delivery.

- Paint a picture to help the reader understand the consequences of your words.

Name
Address
City, State Zip

Date

Bell of Pennsylvania
P.O. Box 8585
Philadephia, PA 19173   Re: (215) 555-2820 (residence)

Dear Sir or Madam:

My phone bill, dated June 7, has charges for calls I didn't make.

The following charges are erroneous:

Apr. 18 9:42 a.m. to Los Angeles (213) 555-7610 34 min.
April 18 10:30 a.m. to Santa Fe   (505) 555-6738 90 min.
April 18 1:10 p.m. to Denver   (303) 555-6833 68 min.

I was at my office from 8:30 a.m. until 5:30 p.m. on April 18. No one else was at my residence on that day.

I will not accept responsibility for these calls. Please delete them from my bill.

Thank you.

Nalini Ranawat

• List the erroneous calls as they appear on your statement.

• Explain why you're not responsible for the charges and direct that they be removed from your bill.

Name
Address
City, State Zip

Date

Mr. Felix Bruno
Spiffy Dry Cleaning
906 Brown Street
Columbus, OH 43215

Dear Felix:

Between tailoring and dry cleaning, I spend about $1,000 a year with you. That means you're willing to forego at least $10,000 to $15,000 in future business, because you won't compensate me for the dress you ruined.

In addition to the revenue you'll lose from me, I'll make it a point to mention to everyone in my club, office and church how you ruined my dress and refused to make good. That can easily extend to another $50,000 in lost business for you every year. That doesn't make you a very good businessperson, Felix.

We both know that accidents happen...and I'd like to think that I'm dealing with reputable businesspeople who take responsibility for them when they do.

Your refusal to pay me for my unwearable dress is going to cost you a lot more than it will cost me to replace it.

Sincerely,

Donna Guerrero

- Although the seeming purpose of this letter is simply to tell an unresponsive business-person that they will lose business, it may also stir him to make restitution when the potential loss is indicated in black and white.

- Don't threaten legal action when it's obvious to the injuring party there will be none (owner's loss is too insignificant).

Name
Address
City, State Zip

Date

Ms. Jennifer Waters
Manager
The Alouette
1300 Pearson Place
San Francisco, CA 94121

Dear Ms. Waters:

I've always enjoyed staying at the Alouette, but if room service remains as slow as it was during my stay last week, I won't return.

I had a 50-minute wait for breakfast one morning, and over an hour's wait another morning. In both cases, I had placed my order the night before to avoid delays. And my request for coffee during one afternoon meeting was never met.

I'm willing to pay top dollar for top service, but I resent paying for this kind of performance. May I have your assurance that the problem will be resolved? If not, I'll have no choice but to stay at another hotel when I'm in San Francisco.

Sincerely,

Helene Acheson

- Service establishments appreciate being told of problem areas. You're doing them a favor by being straightforward.

- Indicate what you plan to do if the hotel doesn't take action.

Name
Address
City, State Zip

Date

Mr. Eric B. Sweeney
General Manager
Conniff's Department Store
Herald Plaza
Madison, WI 53707

Dear Mr. Sweeney:

Trying to shop in your store is a frustrating experience.

Why? Because there are never any salespeople around. Yesterday I waited ten minutes for service in the housewares department before throwing my hands up and leaving the store. I lost my patience, and Conniff's lost a $98.00 purchase.

This wasn't an isolated experience. On several occasions I've had to scout up salespeople to ring up my purchases. There's hardly ever a salesperson in sight.

I've continued to shop at Conniff's because I like your merchandise and your prices. But now I'm questioning whether it's worth the effort.

If you'd like to keep a disgruntled customer from becoming a former customer, hire some more salespeople.

Very truly yours,

Noelle Ritchie

- Cite a specific example of your complaint.

- Warn the reader that they will lose a good customer if the service doesn't improve.

Name
Address
City, State Zip

Date

Mr. Nessim Saltes
Little Istanbul Restaurant
3900 Seventh Street
New York, NY 10022

Dear Mr. Saltes:

My wife is confined to a wheelchair. To avoid uncomfortable
situations, I always call ahead to be certain a facility can accommodate handicapped people.

Can you imagine our surprise—after being told that your restaurant had handicapped access—when we arrived and found that
the access was through a delivery entrance? Can you understand
why I was angry and why my wife felt humiliated? Offering to
have her wheeled through the kitchen into the dining area does
not constitute compliance with the Americans with Disabilities Act.

In addition to the embarrassment you caused us, I wonder if you
have any idea of the fines you're risking with your non-compli-
ance. I plan to help you find out, because I'm filing a formal
complaint against your restaurant.

Sincerely,

Adam Baldwin

- Letters are great for blowing off steam and for helping people understand their obligations.

- In many ways, a "threat" on paper has more power than a verbal confrontation. Use
your pen to confirm your rights under the law.

Name
Address
City, State Zip

Date

Mr. Kevin Jonczak
Best Value Appliances
5420 Commerce Avenue
Irving, TX 75261

Dear Mr. Jonczak:

I'm disappointed by your unwillingness to make good on the defective television you sold to me.

I'm tired of the delays and puzzled by your unresponsiveness. Your delivery man acknowledged that the console was damaged (see copy of my receipt), and I want a replacement unit or a refund in full.

If you ignore this letter as you have my calls, I'll take this issue directly to your store manager. Let's get it resolved, shall we? You need to live up to your "satisfaction guaranteed" motto.

I'll expect your call within the week.

Sincerely,

Edwin Holt

- Don't just call when you have problems. Create a "paper trail" that proves you attempted to communicate.

- Be clear as to subsequent action if your complaint is not acted upon. And be prepared to follow through.

Name
Address
City, State Zip

Date

Mr. Alton Lister
Store Manager
Best Value Appliance
5420 Commerce Avenue
Irving, TX 75261

Dear Mr. Lister:

I'm sorry to have to ask you to handle a transaction that your salesperson, Kevin Jonczak, should be taking care of, but I don't have any choice. He won't answer my calls or correspondence.

I want a replacement for the defective television I purchased from your store. It was delivered with a large gouge on the side of the console. As you'll see from the attached copy of my receipt, your deliveryman acknowledged the problem. All I'm asking you to do is give me what I paid for: a television in perfect condition.

If you can give me a delivery date for the new television, and an approximate delivery time, I'll be sure that someone is home to receive it. Call me during the day at (304) 555-3900 or in the evening at (304) 555-4896.

Sincerely,

Edwin Holt

P.S. Mr. Jonczak needs a refresher course on customer service. He's not serving the best interests of your store with his evasive and non-responsive attitude.

- Let the manager know that you have been trying to "go through proper channels" without success.

- Ask for a delivery schedule to emphasize your expectations.

Name
Address
City, State Zip

Date

Mr. W. E. Bunting
President
Best Value Appliances
Triboro Towers/Suite 600
Phoenix, AZ 85052

Dear Mr. Bunting:

The Best Value Appliances store in Irving, Texas has failed to live up to—or acknowledge—your satisfaction-guaranteed pledge.

I'm seeking a replacement for the damaged television that was delivered to me two months ago. As shown on the enclosed copy of my delivery receipt, the driver noted that the television was damaged in transit. In retrospect, I'm sorry I accepted delivery because the personnel at your Irving store have ignored my numerous calls and letters (copies enclosed), and I'm stuck with a defective set.

I'm ready to go to the local media to vent my displeasure with Best Value. My hope, however, is that you'll make that step unnecessary. I'd appreciate a call from you or a representative to let me know when I can expect a replacement unit. I can be reached during the day at (304) 555-3900, or in the evening at (304) 555-4896.

I expect a call by March 12. Thanks for your expected intercession.

Sincerely,

Edwin Holt

- Don't lose your rational tone or *you'll* be perceived to be the problem. Keep the focus on the store as the villain.

- Define your expectations and provide a deadline.

Name
Address
City, State Zip

Date

Director
Texas Consumer Protection Agency
1112 Eliot Street
Austin, TX 78613

Dear Sir or Madam:

This is a formal complaint against the Best Value store in Irving, Texas.

I purchased a Nakamura console television in December. When it was delivered, the driver acknowledged on the receipt that there was damage on the side of the cabinet (a copy of the receipt is enclosed). I accepted the set, assuming that Best Value would make good, as promised. They've stonewalled me, disavowing any responsibility for the defect (see enclosed correspondence).

After four months of trying to settle this issue with unreasonable people, I'm turning to you for help. I want a replacement for my damaged television. And I'd like to see you take punitive action against Best Value to "send them a message" that this sort of irresponsible behavior will not be tolerated.

If you need more information before proceeding, you can reach me during the day at (304) 555-3900, or in the evening at (304) 555-4896.

Very truly yours,

Edwin Holt

• Most states have a consumer protection unit that will assist you. Put your tax dollars to work for yourself!

• Briefly explain the situation and tell what action you expect.

Name
Address
City, State Zip

Date

Mr. Chester Garfield
Regional Manager
Spirit Rover, Inc.
1782 Warwick Road, Suite 610
Chicago, IL 60602

Dear Mr. Garfield:

It's obvious Pitcairn Motors, in Skokie, has no intention of making good on a bad car. Here's the sequence of events that's forced me to turn to you for help:

1. I drove my brand-new Spirit Rover out of Pitcairn's lot on March 3. Within one mile, the radiator exploded.
2. After waiting a week for the dealer to make the necessary repairs, I had the car for five more days when the electrical system caught fire.
3. After another week of Rent-a-Wreck, I anxiously took possession of my car again and, within two weeks, had a cracked engine block.

The dealer is now suggesting that I'm the problem, not the car. Before I go to the time and trouble of contacting attorneys and consumer agencies, I'm asking you for help. I want the new car that I paid for, not the lemon that's now sitting in the dealer's service bay.

Call me at my office at (312) 555-9339, or in the evening at (708) 555-1473. I'd like to reach an understanding by next week. I can't be without a car much longer.

With great anticipation,

Marshall Glen

• Regional offices are usually more responsive than local dealers. Turn to them whenever a serious issue arises.

• Explain what future actions will be taken if there is no satisfaction. It helps the negotiation.

Name
Address
City, State Zip

Date

Mr. Harold Denkenberg
WPVT Action News
1900 Allison Bay Parkway
Boston, MA 02109

Dear Mr. Denkenberg:

A red flag should have gone up when HomePride Construction gave me a price for siding that was 50% lower than its closest competitor. However, the combination of a tempting price and a persuasive salesperson sold me on the deal.

The workmanship was beyond shoddy. After the first rain, a number of panels fell off and many others shifted, exposing insulation underneath. Armed with my 25-year guarantee, I've called HomePride several times a week for two months, but no one will agree to make the repairs.

If you come out to my home, you'll see for yourself how HomePride has turned the exterior into a nightmare. I'll also show you their 25-year guarantee and their pie-in-the-sky literature.

I think you'll find this is a great visual story that will help many homeowners avoid a similar fate...and it should also have great ratings appeal, because every homeowner can relate to it. I'm usually home during the day, and you can reach me at (617) 555-5229. May I hear from you?

Sincerely,

Connie Stanger

- You need to offer visual images such as fallen siding, exposed weatherproofing and written guarantee when attempting to get television coverage.

- Remember: ratings determine coverage. Indicate why you think your problem will draw viewers.

Name
Address
City, State Zip

Date

Mr. Matthew George
Bilt-Rite Furniture
2770 Montgomery Avenue
Flagstaff, AZ 86001

Dear Mr. George:

Unless you'd like to have a conversation with the State Attorney General, I had better find a check for $1,015 in my mailbox by June 10. That will be exactly six months to the day that you picked up your defective sofa.

To be sure you have the whole story, here's a recap:

o   I purchased a sofa from Bilt-Rite on October 15, and gave a $300 deposit.
o   The sofa was delivered on November 28, and I paid the balance of $715.
o   On November 29, I called my salesperson when I realized that the fabric on the pillows and frame was from different dye lots.
o   The salesperson (Lois Waters) assured me that the sofa would be fixed within 30 days. Eleven days later it was picked up, and ever since I've received nothing but lies and evasions.

You've created an empty spot in my living room, a hole in my wallet, and a knot in my stomach. Now I'd like to return the favor. If I don't have my complete refund by June 10, I'll do what I should have done months ago, and report you to the State Attorney General.

Sincerely,

Ruth Tremont

• Explain your position right up front.

• Summarize key dates and actions.

```
                              Name
                             Address
                         City, State Zip

Date


Ms. Ellen Monte
Better Business Bureau of Orange County
3812 Willow Brook Street
Tustin, CA 92680


Dear Ms. Monte:
```

We were badgered and insulted by a regional representative of the Child Achievement Encyclopedia Company here in Tustin. We're contemplating legal action, but we also want your agency to warn other unsuspecting potential customers.

We inquired about the Child Achievement Encyclopedia and agreed (reluctantly) to have a salesperson visit our home. The sales call was a nightmare.

We couldn't get the representative, who called himself "Mr. Smith," to leave. We kept insisting we needed time to think about such an expensive purchase ($1,200). He actually had the gall to say that we seemed unconcerned about the future of our child.

After two hours of browbeating, my husband said we didn't want the encyclopedia. That's when Mr. Smith demanded that we give him $50 for his time. When I picked up the phone to call the police, he gathered his materials and left.

This company needs to be put out of business. Please tell us what steps you plan to take.

Sincerely,

Mary Secord

- Don't be coy. Situations like these call for strong language.

- Detail your specific objections and expectations.

Cancellation of Door-to-Door Purchase (2-38)

Name
Address
City, State Zip

Date

Ms. Elena Todd
Stay-Right Adjustable Beds, Inc.
133 N. Henry Avenue
Richmond, VA 23231   Re: Cancellation of contract

Dear Ms. Todd:

We've decided to take advantage of the "cooling-off period" provided by federal law, and we're canceling the purchase we made last evening of a Stay-Right adjustable bed.

In accordance with the rights guaranteed by the Federal Trade Commission, we expect to have our deposit refunded within 10 days, and the agreement for extended credit terms destroyed.

We'd appreciate your prompt attention to this request.

Sincerely,

Lois and Frank Sapanaro

- The Federal Trade Commission provides consumer protection through a 3-day cooling off period, during which a door-to-door sale may be cancelled.

- By specifically citing the sponsoring government agency and repayment terms, you demonstrate awareness of your rights and your willingness to fight for them.

Name
Address
City, State Zip

Date

Mail Preference Service
Direct Marketing Association
P.O. Box 9008
Farmingdale, NY 11735

To Whom It May Concern:

Please have my name and address deleted from all mailing lists. I
do not wish to receive unsolicited mail.

Thank you for your attention.

Sincerely,

Rebecca Denney

- Contact the organization listed above if you wish to have your name removed from all mailing lists.

- If you wish to remove your name from just one mailing list, write to the individual mailer.

Congratulations 3

A congratulatory note can add so much to an occasion worth celebrating. It gives the reader the "fifteen minutes of fame" that everyone is entitled to at least once in a lifetime.

Sending a congratulatory letter presents the writer as a magnanimous, aware individual. These qualities will serve you well in both your personal and professional life.

Remember that your letter should be about the *recipient*—not about you. Stifle the impulse to talk about yourself, and direct the spotlight where it belongs—on the reader.

Congratulations on event.   Events such as birthdays, anniversaries, births, and the purchase of a new home warrant congratulations. Your congratulatory letter should be upbeat, warm, and as intimate as the relationship itself. Take this opportunity to say all the nice things that you've been storing up over the years.

Congratulations on achievement.   After working hard to achieve a goal or to overcome an obstacle, everyone appreciates a pat on the back. Use a congratulatory letter to tell the reader that they deserve the good things that have come their way. Be specific in praising them for their accomplishments, and express your conviction that today's brimming cup of cheer will spill over into the future.

Saying it with a poem.   If you have a whimsical mindset, putting your congratulations in the form of a poem can be as entertaining to write as it is to read. It doesn't require a talent for perfect rhyme and meter—the recipient will probably give you an 'A' just for effort, rather than judging your composition on artistic merit.

Name
Address
City, State Zip

Date

Dear Mandy and Howard,

What a relief! All of us at the office had been watching the calendar every day, awaiting word that your bundle of joy had finally arrived. He's already got a built-in fan club!

I understand that he has your bright blue eyes, Mandy, and your curly dark hair, Howard, and that he's beautiful. With your genetic combination, how could he be otherwise?

I am thrilled for all three of you, and especially glad that Howard survived labor and delivery without anesthesia!

Congratulations! I can't wait to get a firsthand look at the little one.

Love,

Cara

- This is a momentous, upbeat occasion. Let your words reflect that you share the joy.

- New parents feel that their baby is the most special person in the world. Your message should affirm that.

Name
Address
City, State Zip

Date

Dear Wendy and Ira,

We're so happy for you! There's nothing quite like the joy of sharing your lives with a child. And we can't think of two people who will make better parents.

As delighted as we are for you, we're even more delighted for baby Michelle. She's lucky to have two wonderful, loving people like you to raise her.

Congratulations and good health. Send photos!

All our love,

Aileen and Mark

- Treat the adoption of a baby as you would any new arrival. A baby is a baby.

- It's a confidence-builder to tell parents that you feel the baby is lucky to have them.

Name
Address
City, State Zip

Date

Dear Rebecca,

I think you and George belong on my roster of great couples:

Antony and Cleopatra
Lunt and Fontanne
Wilma and Fred
Rebecca and George

It may sound corny, but I've always thought you belonged together. That's why I'm delighted that you're engaged. Best wishes for a blissful marriage.

Fondly,

Harry McLaughlin

- Acknowledge that this is a special occasion and that the engaged pair is a special couple.

- Traditionally, "best wishes" are offered to the woman; "congratulations" are offered to the man.

Name
Address
City, State Zip

Date

Dear Ava and Victor,

The news of your marriage has made me so happy and so smug. You've confirmed what I realized as soon as you met—that you belonged together.

I knew you'd make a great couple. You complement each other perfectly!

I wish you a lifetime of love and joy.

Your wise friend,

Marianna

- Include something that makes your wishes unique, instead of the cliched "I hope you'll be very happy together."

- Let the tone of the message convey warmth.

Name
Address
City, State Zip

Date

Dear Madelyn and Dave,

When you two met and married as young kids, you probably gave no thought to becoming a statistic. Yet here you are, defying the odds by staying happily married for 35 years.   You have the envy and the admiration of all your friends.

As wonderful as you are as individuals, you're even more remarkable as a couple. We wish you many more years of marital harmony and the blessing of good health so you can enjoy them.

All our love,

Kitty and Stan

• Recognize that having a long-lasting and successful marriage is an accomplishment.

• Offer the couple your best wishes for the continuation of their happiness.

Name
Address
City, State Zip

Date

Dear Michael,

After watching your bar mitzvah ceremony, it became clear why it's considered a rite of passage into manhood. You were so sure of yourself and so confident of your reading from the scriptures. You related so well to the congregation that no one could ever think of you as a child again. It's obvious how much preparation you put into your bar mitzvah, and that's the mark of a mature, determined person.

I've always known you had great talent and intelligence, and now I know you have the discipline to apply those gifts. I'm so pleased to see that you have what it takes to be successful in whatever you do.

I'm proud of you, Michael. Congratulations.

With love,

Uncle Max

- A follow-up letter after the event has dramatic impact.

- Be specific in your praise, rather than just saying, "You did a wonderful job."

Name
Address
City, State Zip

Date

Dear Norm,

Face it. The time has come when you're going to have to confront some really difficult decisions:

Whether to wake up early or sleep in.

Whether to go sailing or hiking.

Whether to paint a picture or a room.

Whether to watch a movie or a sunset.

You've got some tough choices ahead, Norm. I hope you thoroughly enjoy every one of them.

Congratulations on your retirement.

Sincerely,

Gaby Royce

• Convey a sense of unlimited options to the reader.

• A little humor gets the message across.

Name
Address
City, State Zip

Date

Dear Serena and Keith,

Buying a new home is a combination of joy and jitters. Don't let the former be overshadowed by the latter.

May your housewarming be the first of many celebrations at 6 Carriage Way.

Congratulations and best wishes,

Barry Sykes

- Acknowledge the significance of the event.

- Express a positive outlook for the future.

Name
Address
City, State Zip

Date

Dear Julie,

We wish we had the organizational skills that you possess. Not only did you graduate with honors, you were also the school's sports and yearbook photographer. And you worked after school and on weekends! How did you do it?

We've been lucky to have someone like you as a neighbor. It's been a treat to watch you grow and mature into a wonderful young woman. It's so obvious to us that you have a bright future ahead of you.

Congratulations on your graduation. We're very, very proud of you.

Fondly,

Connie and Marty Cleary

• Comment on the positive characteristics of the graduate.

• Indicate that the future will be rewarding.

Name
Address
City, State Zip

Date

Dear Kirby,

Your hard work paid off—congratulations! Waiting for college acceptance letters can be agonizing, but when they arrive—what a high!

You probably feel lucky that Wesleyan chose you. I see it from a different perspective: Wesleyan is lucky to have you.

Enjoy your college career.

Sincerely,

Joyce Mohr

- Recognize the accomplishment.

- Acknowledge that the reader earned it.

Name
Address
City, State Zip

Date

Dear Serena,

Like many of life's milestones, graduation is a paradox: It signifies a beginning and an end.

As you look back on your past and anticipate your future, I offer enthusiastic congratulations. You've achieved a history of academic excellence and you've established yourself as a person who's willing to take risks.

I'm confident that your diligence and determination will bring you great success and satisfaction.

Good Luck!

Sincerely,

Michael Teiper

• Be specific, if you can, about special accomplishments, such as academic excellence.

• Express optimism for the graduate's future.

Name
Address
City, State Zip

Date

Dear Chuck,

I have always thought of doctors as being 50ish, dignified, and very wise. But now you come along and get a medical degree. I guess I'm going to have to rethink my image of physicians.

Seriously, Chuck, I'm really proud of you. And here's the ultimate compliment: I'll become one of your patients as soon as you open your practice. I can't think of anyone I'd trust more with my health.

I wish you much success, Dr. Cooper. Congratulations!

Affectionately,

Stephanie

- Generally, good natured humor is appropriate and appreciated among friends.

- Be sure to balance the humor with sincere praise.

Name
Address
City, State Zip

Date

Mr. Daniel Michaels
Bachman Insurance Agency
5842 Walker Road
Clayton, MO 63105

Dear Dan:

Whoever said, "Change is the only thing that offers new opportunity," must have been thinking of you. And so am I.

I'm excited and happy for you. And I think your new employer will be, too, when that fertile mind of yours starts to plow some new profits for them.

I know you have some reservations about changing careers at this stage, but I'm sure you'll come to feel at home in the insurance industry in no time at all. Congratulations and success.

Cordially,

Jennifer Hartman

- Starting with a quote adds a fresh element to any letter.

- Make it clear that you feel the new employer has made a wise decision.

Name
Address
City, State Zip

Date

Mr. Sean Gerson
Vice President
The Pennwood Corporation
1223 Stanhope Street
Riverlea, OH 43085

Dear Sean:

I can't begin to tell you how happy I am for you. You worked for
your new position, you waited for it, and when the opportunity
presented itself you were ready for it.

When you have a moment or two to sit back and relax, I hope
you'll have a sip of the enclosed and toast your continuing
success. Congratulations and good luck.

Cordially,

David Newton

- Let the individual know you realize how much this means to them.

- Enclosing something that signifies a celebration (for example, champagne or flowers) is
  a nice touch that will be remembered.

Name
Address
City, State Zip

Date

Dear Mandy,

Even though there are 50 pounds less of you to love, you're still my favorite niece! You look sensational, but more importantly, you've added years to your life.

You've given me the incentive to lose some weight. Following your sensible diet, I'm going to try to muster some will power to start eating healthier foods myself.

I'm proud of you.

With love,

Uncle Charles

- People whose appearance has changed for the better are always pleased when the improvement is noticed.

- Let the person know that it's not just their appearance that's important to you.

Name
Address
City, State Zip

Date

Dear Warren,

That loud sound you might have heard the other evening was a huge sigh of relief.

What great news! When Anita called to let me know that your surgery had been successful, it seemed as if a dark cloud that had been following me around had suddenly vanished.

Do us all a favor, will you? Do what the doctor says and take care of yourself. I'm looking forward to many more years of friendship with you.

I'll see you as soon as you're ready for visitors.

Fondly,

Kenny

- When someone is recovering from major surgery, it's comforting to know that people really care. Take the time to write; it will be greatly appreciated.

- Don't get into medical war stories. Stay upbeat.

Name
Address
City, State Zip

Date

Dear Juliet,

Congratulations on the grand opening of "Jewels by Juliet."

Your designs have been the rage of the neighborhood for years. It's about time your jewelry was available to a larger audience.

Your drive and creativity guarantee success. And your friends will help on the marketing side: We're already boasting that we've been wearing "Jewels by Juliet" for years!

Best of Luck!

Fondly,

Brenda Mikochik

• Express an optimistic attitude regarding the reader's potential for success.

• Back it up with specific positive references to the person's skills.

Name
Address
City, State Zip

Date

Dear Zack,

Every time I was a little lazy—with schoolwork, sports, household chores—my mother would wag her finger at me and say, "If you want to eat the nut, you have to crack the shell."

That bit of wisdom sums up the sensational campaign you ran to become City Council President. Sometimes it seemed as if you were in three sections of the city at the same time. You out-worked (and out-thought) your opponent, Zack.

You may be knee-deep in shells, but now you have the entire municipal streets department to clean up behind you! Congratulations on a much-deserved, hard-fought election. I'm proud to be your friend.

Sincerely,

Stan Nowicki

• No one wins an election without a lot of work. Let the reader know that the effort didn't go unnoticed.

• Quoting someone can often make your point more emphatically. Acquire a book or two of great quotations, and have thousands at your disposal. And you can supplement those with sayings that have been part of your own history.

Name
Address
City, State Zip

Date

Dear Martha,

I love to hear your speeches and have often told you so. But you're so quick to pass off compliments as just flattery.

However, your recent award as Communicator of the Year is tangible proof of your ability as an orator. The Fairfield County Association of Public Speakers is a prestigious organization. And knowing how tough the competition was should add to your pride and satisfaction.

I congratulate you on this outstanding achievement.

With admiration,

Judith Maguire

- Acknowledge the person's talents.

- Point to the prestige of the award or quality of the competition that was faced.

Name
Address
City, State Zip

Date

Dear Harley,

Hear! Hear! Congrats and Whoopdedo!
Salud! Hip Hip Hooray!
All hail! Best Wishes! Bully, too!
Yeah, man! Hot dog! Ole!
You really are a clever chap!
Three cheers! Thumbs up! Oh boy!
You hit the mark; you sank the putt.
You earned it, now enjoy!

Love,

Genevieve

• Be as enthusiastic as you care to be for a congratulatory poem. Whatever the occasion, it's a happy one.

Name
Address
City, State Zip

Date

Dear Gloria and Gary,

After years of resisting the urge,
I hear that you're right on the verge
Of a ring and a kiss
And marital bliss.
What great news—you've decided to merge!

Love,

Annette and Edgar

• Your message should convey that you're 100% in favor of the step the reader is taking.

Name
Address
City, State Zip

Date

Dear Cheryl and Mark,

In charting a course that's harmonious,
Avoid using words acrimonious.
Let giving and taking
And frequent lovemaking
Be guides for your ship "Matrimonious."

Congratulations on your marriage!

Love,

Arlyn and Gene

• You can use some "poetic license" in your wording (for example, "Matrimonius") to add warmth and humor to your message.

Name
Address
City, State Zip

Date

Dear Sarah and Marshall,

Who's sent to you from heaven?
Who's dressed in blue—not pink?
Who's held so tight?
Who cries all night?
Who oftentimes can stink?

Who's Sarah's little treasure?
Who's Marshalls's pride and joy?
Who's love and bliss
And a sloppy kiss?
Your bouncing baby boy!

Congratulations from
All your pals at work

• Parents are usually so delighted with their new arrival that it's hard to over do a "new baby" congratulatory message.

Name
Address
City, State Zip

Date

Dear Jamie,

We knew that you could do it,
With awards you would come through it,
Making parents, friends and relatives so proud.
The diploma's in your hand,
Life's ahead, it should be grand,
For a girl who stands so far above the crowd!

Love,

Aunt Sylvia and Uncle Wayne

• Recognize the achievement and be positive about the future.

Name
Address
City, State Zip

Date

Dear Amy and John,

A mortgage
A mailbox
A lawn
And a mower;
A washer
A dryer
A dog
A leaf blower.

Then a basement
That's wet
And a crack
In a beam.
Get set
To enjoy
The American Dream!

All kidding aside, homeownership is wonderful. Welcome to the ranks!

Love,

Carol and Doug

• A little irony is okay, as long as it's presented with a sense of humor.

Name
Address
City, State Zip

Date

Dear Christina,

You're newly relocated,
And much remunerated.
Upon the fastest track you have no peer.
I know you'll be successful,
Though the challenge will be stressful.
Kudos on your illustrious career!

Good Luck on Your New Job!

Sincerely,

Greta

• Everyone's nervous and excited about starting a new job. Build confidence when you congratulate the reader.

Name
Address
City, State Zip

Date

Dear Steven,

The boss says that you're number one;
A whiz who can get the job done.
All those hours of devotion
Have earned you a promotion.
Your climb to the top has begun!

Congratulations!

Warmly,

Lawrence Needleman

• Show that the boss is not the only one who recognizes the reader's accomplishments.

Correspondence to Family and Friends 4

When it comes to communicating by letter with family and friends, *you're* the best judge of what to say and how to say it. Each relationship is unique, so heed your internal barometer when deciding which topics are appropriate, how much information you want to share, and the degree of intimacy that's comfortable for you and for the reader.

Letters to your parents. Sometimes it's easier to communicate by letter than it is face to face. This is especially true with sensitive issues. Perhaps you've totalled the car. Writing a letter gives you the opportunity to compose your thoughts and deliver your news without fear of interruption (You what??!!), or verbal assault (How could you be so stupid??!!). A letter also gives the reader the extra time required to react to disappointing news and cool down before the next communication with you. Communicating bad news by letter isn't the coward's way out—it's simply a wise approach when emotions could be volatile.

If your letter contains negative news, a few sentences at the beginning of the letter should prepare the reader for what's to follow. Next, relate the information as clearly as possible, taking responsibility for your actions if you've caused the problem. Then state your intention to rectify the situation, and describe a plan and time frame in which you intend to carry it out.

If you're delivering news that you're happy about (Guess what? I eloped with a rodeo clown last weekend!), but believe will meet with the reader's disapproval, state your conviction that the decision has been well thought out and is the right one for *you*.

Good news. The good news letter is fun to write. It gives the author a chance to take a bow, take some credit, and accentuate the positive. Convey the information, share your feelings about it, and describe how you think it will affect your future. If possible, try to make the reader feel a sense of reflected glory.

Bad news. There's really no juxtaposition of words that can make bad news sound good. The first few sentences of your letter should gently alert the reader to unhappy tidings. Deliver the news candidly, but avoid unnecessary embellishments. If the reader can help in some way, describe how. Try to end the letter on a philosophical note.

Reminders. The reminder letter should be polite, but firm. State your position, your justification, and your expectation. In some cases, it's also necessary to describe the steps you'll take if the reminder doesn't produce results.

Holiday correspondence. Holidays provide the opportunity to put positive feelings about our lives and our relationship in writing so that those who care about us can share in them. Make the message positive, uplifting and optimistic. Holiday letters should spread warmth and cheer. Any bad news should be saved for a separate letter.

Name
Address
City, State Zip

Date

Dear Mom and Dad,

I wish I could rewind my life like a videotape. Then I could start the last semester over and study harder, receive better grades, and not have to write this letter.

Unfortunately, I have to face reality, and that means admitting that my grades were awful. I'm angry with myself for not doing better. I guess I put my social life and campus activities ahead of hitting the books.

I'm making a renewed commitment to apply myself next semester. I know I have the potential to earn good grades, and seeing how awful it feels to do poorly, I won't shortchange myself again.

Love,

Jerry

- Don't make excuses. Take responsibility for your bad grades.

- State your commitment to improve.

Name
Address
City, State Zip

Date

Dear Mom and Dad,

I was pretty cocky when I left home. I remember saying that I couldn't wait to be on my own.

Now I know that the reality of independence isn't as picture-perfect as the fantasy. The truth is, I'm not happy here, and I need a little time to think about my future. It would be great to be able to do that thinking in familiar surroundings.

That's why I want to come home. I need your support while I sort things out. I'm willing to get a job, and I'll certainly help around the house. I'll even cook. Just tell me its OK to move back home for a while.

Your loving daughter,

Briana

- Explain why you want to move back home.

- State your intention to contribute to the household in some way.

Name
Address
City, State Zip

Date

Dear Mom and Dad,

I've taken a major step in my personal life, and I want to share it with you.

For about three months, I've been dating a man I met at school. His name is Jonathan Merbrook, and he comes from Atlanta. He's a psychology major, too, so we have a lot in common.

Our relationship has become serious and, after much discussion, we've decided to live together. We both believe that it's the right thing to do, and we're looking forward to spending more time together.

I hope you'll support me in my decision.

Love,

Beverly

- Give some pertinent information about the live-in.

- Indicate that the decision wasn't made impetuously.

Name
Address
City, State Zip

Date

Dear Mom and Dad,

You taught me by example that a good marriage is life's greatest reward. That's why I promised myself that when I met the right person I would make the same commitment you two made.

Well, I met her and I kept my promise. Her name is Laura Patten, and we were married at City Hall on January 15.

Here's what you should know about her: she's 27, she's a graphic artist, she grew up in Chicago, she plays the clarinet and she's got a wonderful sense of humor.

We're so much in love, we just couldn't wait to get married, but I want you to meet Laura just as soon as we can get a few days off to travel home.

Laura and I are living at my place until we find a bigger apartment.

Mom and Dad, you were right—marriage is life's greatest reward!

Love,

Simon

- Let the readers feel that they contributed to your positive attitude toward marriage.

- Reassure them that you're confident you made the right decision.

Name
Address
City, State Zip

Date

Dear Mom and Dad,

I've just gotten some very disturbing news, and I need your support.

I'm pregnant. I didn't plan it, and I don't know what to do about it. The baby's father isn't willing to make a commitment to me or his future child.

Whatever I decide to do will have enormous implications for my future, so I want to consider all my options. I'd really appreciate some advice.

No lectures, please. Just let me know what you think. I can't promise to do what you suggest, but I certainly promise to listen.

Love,

Jennie

- Acknowledge the significance of the circumstances.

- Ask for support.

Name
Address
City, State Zip

Date

Dear Mom and Dad,

I'm conscientious about money and, generally, I manage it well. But this past month I've encountered unforeseen expenses, and my bank account is depleted.

I need $200 to cover my outstanding debts. I would have preferred dealing with this problem myself, but I don't have the resources.

Could you please send me the money? I'll repay you as soon as I can.

Thanks.

Gratefully,

Bob

- Reassure the reader that your financial situation is the result of unusual circumstances, not reckless spending.

- Be straightforward about how much money you need.

Name
Address
City, State Zip

Date

Dear Mom and Dad,

Every time you asked if I had a girlfriend yet; every time you questioned why this cousin or that friend was getting married and I wasn't; every time you asked aloud if I'd ever give you grand-children...every single time, I wondered if you knew.

I think it's time I ended the speculation: Yes, I'm gay. I assume that this declaration simply confirms suspicions you've had for many years. And I also assume that our relationship won't change in any way.

I want your continued love and support.

All my love,

Greg

- Suggest that your parents may have suspected the truth.

- Make it clear that, as far as you're concerned, nothing about your relationship with your parents should change.

Name
Address
City, State Zip

Date

Dear Dawn,

I never believed in the phrase "happily ever after." It seemed so corny and naive. I certainly didn't think it would ever apply to me.

That was before I became engaged! Now I'm convinced of my everlasting happiness with the most wonderful man.

His name is Stuart Renshaw. He's an architect. He's smart, funny and sexy. We met about a year ago through mutual friends and have been together ever since.

We're planning a huge May wedding. Expect an invitation!

Love,

Rae Anne

- Share some pertinent information about your fiance or fiancee.

- Give some indication of the kind of wedding you're planning, such as, "We're planning a huge wedding," "We're planning to elope to Tahiti," etc.

I Got Married (4-09)

Name
Address
City, State Zip

Date

Dear Brenda,

You know I've been dreaming about my wedding day for years, and I finally got to hear those wedding bells ring.

Seth and I made a decision to elope on Valentine's Day. We flew to Las Vegas and got married in one of those little chapels you always hear about. It was so tacky and romantic—the perfect setting for our offbeat relationship.

All our belongings are piled in boxes in our new townhouse on Lakeshore Drive. We're still in shock at the idea of actually co-habiting <u>legally</u>.

The truth is, I'm happy. Seth's happy. And I hope my lifelong friend will be happy for us.

Love,

Georgeanna

• Share some details of when and how the wedding took place.

• Transmit the joy that you're feeling.

Name
Address
City, State Zip

Date

Dear Ian,

My perseverance has paid off. On September 16 I became managing editor of childrens' books for Holiday Publishing!

I'm now a full-fledged New Yorker with a studio apartment in Manhattan. It's a short walk to work (or a cab ride in the rain). After months of financial uncertainty, I'm indulging myself. I've even enrolled in a health club.

I'm amazed at how my situation has reversed itself. The job search was a learning experience that proved the value of determination and staying power. It also proved the value of supportive friends like you. Thanks.

Fondly,

Marsha

P.S. My new home phone number is (212) 555-2872

• Give some details, rather than just the bare bones, of your new situation.

• If the reader was helpful or supportive during your job search, express your appreciation.

Name
Address
City, State Zip

Date

Dear Margaret,

I'm approaching the end of this month with a mixture of anticipation and disbelief. Can it be forty-two years since I taught my first sixth grade class? The calendar says yes, which is why I'm about to become a retired schoolteacher.

I plan to take full advantage of my year-round independence. I'm already researching a winetasting tour of France for September. Would you be interested in joining me?

And while I watch my garden grow this summer, I'm going to try my hand at writing a few short stories that have been simmering on my brain's back burner for years.

I'm looking forward to this new passage. As long as my health remains good, I feel ready to tackle anything.

The school is throwing a retirement party for me on June 23. The sixth graders are even composing an original song! I've been given "carte blanche" to invite friends and relatives, so I hope you'll come—I may need some "bucking up."

Give me a call and let me know if you can make it.

Kindest regards,

Mary Phelps

- Tell the reader how it feels to be approaching retirement.

- Share your plans and aspirations. If you're looking for companionship, say so.

Name
Address
City, State Zip

Date

Dear Uncle Bart,

Wasn't it you who always proposed a round of touch football at holiday picnics? Those family free-for-alls were Todd's first introduction to competitive sports.

Since you taught your nephew how to throw a pass, you deserve some of the glory.

Last weekend, Todd made the winning touchdown for his team in the district play-offs. The Conestoga Pioneers won 14-13, and Todd's jubilant teammates carried him off the field on their shoulders. Now he's a school hero!

Todd's proud, we're proud, and you should be proud, too.

Love,

Laura

- State why you think the reader will be interested in the news.

- Relate some details about the event.

Name
Address
City, State Zip

Date

Dear Danielle,

A miracle has happened. At least that's how I feel.

I'm pregnant! While that announcement may be routine to some people, to Jim and me it's mind-boggling. We're still marveling over it. You know how long we've be trying, and what a difficult time I had conceiving.

The baby is due in October. So far, everything is proceeding according to the pregnancy textbooks, but I'm having amniocentesis next week to be absolutely certain that all is well.

This is all so new and thrilling. We'll keep you posted.

Love,

Jackie

• People love to receive good news. Share your happiness with the reader.

• Tell when the baby is due, and promise to give updates on your progress.

We've Moved (4-14)

Name
Address
City, State Zip

Date

Dear Elsa,

We're celebrating our independence. We no longer have to:

1) Mow an acre of grass every week.

2) Mulch and plant several garden beds each Spring.

3) Weed those gardens when the mulch isn't thick enough.

4) Shovel snow.

5) Rake leaves.

6) Do all our own home repairs.

We've chucked homeownership for the carefree life of lakeside condo ownership. After one month, we've concluded that it was the best decision we've ever made. Relaxation has become a way of life.

We'd love to see you and show you our new quarters. Why not plan to take a drive to Marshall Lake for a visit. Please call us at (404) 555-1058. We'll roll out the red carpet (we have plenty of spare energy now).

Best regards,

Minnie and Al

• Tell the reader what factors affected your decision to move.

• Express how happy you'd be to see an old friend.

Dad Has to Have an Operation (4-15)

Name
Address
City, State Zip

Date

Dear Allan,

Dad has been so active since retiring that I often forget how old he actually is. Recently, however, he's been experiencing shortness of breath. His doctor put him in the hospital for a cardiac catheterization and the results were not good.

His arteries are blocked and he's at risk for a heart attack. Two consulting cardiologists agree that Dad needs a bypass without delay. The surgery will be performed on Friday, April 26 at University Hospital.

Dad's a brave guy, but he's shaken by the prospect of this surgery. There is risk involved, but the doctors seem optimistic. They say that Dad could be back on the golf course in eight weeks.

The operation starts at 8:00 a.m., and could last up to eight hours. Unless you decide to come, I'll phone you as soon as I have news.

Love,

Anne

- Give a reasonably detailed account of the situation so the person doesn't feel uninformed and left out.

- Stress the positive.

Name
Address
City, State Zip

Date

Dear Tom,

I have some sad news to share with you. Grandpa died peacefully yesterday afternoon at about three o'clock. He was sitting in his chair, watching the ocean, when he closed his eyes and slipped away.

He was loved by so many people during his cantankerous eighty-seven years—not the least of whom were his grandchildren. We'll miss playing Trivial Pursuit and Scrabble with him. Even though he'd pound his fist when we beat him, he always loved the challenge.

He had asked to be cremated and to have his ashes scattered over the ocean. I hope you can be there in the spring when the family carries out his wishes.

I'll send more details when they're available.

All my love,

Rita

• When the reader is far away, they need to feel "connected" to the family during a time of loss. Let your words reflect this.

• Let the reader know about plans for a tribute or memorial.

Name
Address
City, State Zip

Date

Dear Stan,

We both know that Dad never seemed close to Aunt Betty. He only saw or spoke to her once or twice a year, and Mom always had to push him to do even that much.

Well, we just received word that Aunt Betty died last night, and amazingly, Dad seems devastated. (That's not an overstatement.) Mom and I think he feels guilty that he didn't stay in closer touch with her.

Anyway, I thought you should know. Dad would probably appreciate hearing from you. In fact, I'd like to hear from you, too. It's been too long.

Hope all is well.

Love,

Jean

- Explaining a situation in honest terms gives the reader the information they need to respond appropriately.

- If you're writing to someone who might not know what is expected of them, suggest a call or letter to comfort the bereaved.

Name
Address
City, State Zip

Date

Dear Tony,

I just had a call from Paul Irwin's dad. He wanted us to know that Paul had a serious heart attack. He's going to survive, but his heart is damaged. In fact, Mr. Irwin said that Paul will require extensive surgery.

It will be at least another week or two until Paul can see anyone, so don't even think about flying in for a while. I'll let you know how things are going. In the meantime, you can send cards or letters to:

Cardiac Unit
City Hospital West
1900 W. Poplar Street
Omaha, NE 68102

I've had no luck trying to reach you by phone, so unless I hear from you, I'll send you written updates as more information becomes available. Incidentally, it might be a nice touch to call Mr. Irwin (402-555-6936). He's lonely and scared.

Let me hear from you.

Best,

Norm

• Offer a mailing address for the sick person.

• If you're the person on the spot, you can be of great service by telling others what to send or do.

Name
Address
City, State Zip

Date

Dear Darryl,

I've always tried to avoid television reports and articles about AIDS. The disease seemed so remote from my world, and I was naive enough to believe that it would never affect me, or anyone close to me.

Now I'm facing the reality that AIDS touches everyone. You probably know that Barry has, for months, been missing a lot of work because of a recurring "flu." Well, last night, he confided to me that he has AIDS. He asked me to share the information with you, but no one else.

I feel certain that he'd appreciate a call or a note from you. Come to think of it, so would I. We need to talk about what we can do to help Barry through the difficult times that lie ahead.

Best always,

Sarah

- There's no way to sugar coat information like this. Don't even try. Just talk about how the situation might best be handled.

- If the information is confidential, be sure to state so clearly.

Name
Address
City, State Zip

Date

Dear Flora,

Even with my absolute faith in the Almighty, this is a day that has severely tested my resolve. Our dear friend, Lorraine, suffered a cerebral hemorrhage early this morning, and died within hours. It was all totally unexpected.

I've spent the last few hours with Ed, helping him with some of the arrangements. He knows how close we all were with Lorraine but, at this point, he's insistent that the services and burial be strictly for the family. If he changes his mind (a possibility, given his current state), I'll call you.

Lorraine was so full of life. It's impossible to believe she's gone. I wish you lived closer; I'd feel so much better if you were here with me.

All my love,

Jacqueline

- Although the news will be shocking wherever you insert it, give the reader a sentence or two to prepare for it.

- Give a brief summary of the circumstances. Details can be dealt with when you talk.

Name
Address
City, State Zip

Date

Dear Sidney,

As I write this letter, it occurs to me what a poor correspondent I've been. I'm embarrassed that I feel compelled to write only when there's bad news.

Aunt Kate was in an automobile accident last week and broke her hip. She'll be in the hospital for a few more days, then she'll be transferred to a rehabilitation center. The recuperation could take several months.

Her spirit needs a boost, and it would be helpful if you wrote or phoned her.

The address is:

Memorial Rehabilitation Center
Room 301
Paoli, PA 19301
Telephone: (215) 555-4989

Thanks, Sidney.

Love from your cousin,

Emily

• Tell the circumstances of the accident and the extent of the injuries.

• State what the reader can do to help.

Name
Address
City, State Zip

Date

Dear Alex,

I've always lived my life without much concern for the future, but at this moment I feel my own mortality.

My Dad passed away last week. Although, as you know, he'd been ill for months, losing him was a shock. I used to visit him every day, and I already miss our talks.

Our family has requested that any contributions in his name be made to the Boy Scouts of America. That's because, in so many ways, Dad was the quintessential scout. The years he spent as a boy scout were the the happiest of his life. And he was the most beloved scout leader imaginable. Throughout his life, he embodied the bravery and loyalty that is the real meaning of scouting.

I hope that to some extent, at least, I'll find a way to follow in his footsteps.

With a heavy heart,

Jake

- There's no need to hide your feelings in a letter of this nature.

- Let the reader know your preference for commemorating the deceased.

Name
Address
City, State Zip

Date

Dear Ellen,

I'm a strong person, but right now I feel my strength is being tested. That's why I need support from you.

Ellen, I lost the baby. Even though my obstetrician says that miscarriages are common with first pregnancies, I have such a feeling of emptiness...and even failure. We wanted this baby so much!

Rather than getting a phone call, I'd appreciate one of your long, newsy letters. When I feel up to talking about this, I'll call you.

Thanks.

Love,

Trudy

- This is a time when you need support. Don't be afraid to ask for it.

- Don't expect the recipient to be a mind reader. Tell them exactly how to help you (notify others, stay in touch with you by letter, etc.).

Name
Address
City, State Zip

Date

Dear Mom and Dad,

Every article I read says that the recession touches everyone.
Now I believe it. Last Friday Jack was laid off. We had heard
rumbles about the plant cutting back, but hoped Jack's outstanding job performance record would protect him. It didn't.

On the bright side, he has a few leads on job possibilities, and we
can manage on my income for a while. I know he won't be out of
work for long, so I'd better not get used to his being home.

Please don't worry about us. We're going to be just fine.

My love to both of you,

Louise

- For the sake of everyone's pride, make it clear that the lay-off was the result of circumstances, not performance.

- Keep the letter upbeat and reassuring, especially if there's nothing the reader can do about the situation.

Name
Address
City, State Zip

Date

Dear Mom and Dad,

As Maureen and I struggled to make a go of our recycling business, I listened to every motivational tape I could get my hands on. The more we fell behind in payments and payroll, the more I listened.

It took me a while, but I finally realized that it takes a lot more than motivation and enthusiasm to run a business. In retrospect, we weren't prepared emotionally, technically or financially to even start this business. I was too naive to know what I didn't know.

We're okay. Don't worry. Maureen already has a good job lined up, and as we're shutting down the business, I've been interviewing for an engineering job. But we both agree that as soon as everything settles down (in other words, when our finances are stabilized), we're going to take another shot at entrepreneurship.

I've borrowed my new motto from Henry Ford. I wrote it in big block letters on poster board, and hung it over our bed: "Failure," said Ford, "is the opportunity to begin again, more intelligently." We'll be back!

All my love,

Chuck

• Taking responsibility for the loss demonstrates maturity and growth (which will be important if you decide to ask for future assistance from relatives!)

• Explain your plans. Don't let the reader wonder how you're faring, or what you'll do.

Name
Address
City, State Zip

Date

Dear Nan and Bill,

You never expect to see people you know on the eleven o'clock news. But there they were—Jim and Judy Benson—being interviewed as their house burned in the background. Fortunately, no one was hurt, but the house was completely destroyed, along with everything else they owned.

I'm heading a drive to help Judy and Jim through this difficult time. Friends are being asked to contribute whatever they can: food, money, clothing (the Benson boys are five and nine), sheets, blankets—whatever! So far the response has been fantastic.

Can I count on your support? Donations can be left at my house any day this week, between 8 A.M. and noon.

My address is: 14 South Remington Rd.
                Manchester
                555-2403

If that's not convenient, someone will stop at your house for a pick-up—just call to set up a time.

Thanks,

Maggie Rosoff

- Some people cannot or will not contribute money. Offer alternatives.

- Make it as easy as possible for people to help out (in this case, by offering to pick up items at their home).

Name
Address
City, State Zip

Date

Dear Anna,

I was going through my closet yesterday, trying to plan what to wear to an upcoming Bar Association dinner. I thought of my black strapless dress with the matching shawl, and spent ten minutes searching for it. Then I remembered that you borrowed it last spring before you moved to Dayton.

Would you please mail it back to me by the end of next week? I have my heart set on wearing it to the dinner, and I need to be sure it still fits.

I'll call you to make sure it's on its way.

Thanks.

Best always,

Amanda

- Telling the reader that you need the item by a specific date creates some urgency without sounding like you're reprimanding.

- Let the borrower know you'll be on their case and won't let the matter drop.

Name
Address
City, State Zip

Date

Dear Arnie,

I feel uncomfortable writing this letter. The subject of money is always an awkward one—especially between friends. But two months have passed since you borrowed a hundred dollars from me, and I'd like to be repaid.

I value our friendship and don't want it to be tarnished by an outstanding debt. Would you please send me the money by the end of the week?

Thanks. I'm confident that I can count on you.

Sincerely,

Leslie

- Tell the reader that you dislike having to ask for your money.

- Set a deadline, and indicate that the friendship is in jeopardy if the deadline isn't met.

Name
Address
City, State Zip

Date

Dear Mitch,

Here's a copy of last month's phone bill. I've circled the calls that I made during your stay here. The remainder are yours. By my calculations you owe $53.21.

The phone bill is due on the 21st so please send a check to arrive by the 15th.

Thanks.

Sincerely,

Glen

- Enclose a copy of the phone bill, indicating the outstanding charges.

- Be clear about your expectations.

```
                          Name
                         Address
                      City, State Zip

     Date

     Dear Maggie,

     I'm thankful that we've agreed to share the burden of Grandma's
     care.  And I've actually enjoyed having her with us. But after
     fulfilling my six months' obligation, I'm ready for a break.  It's not
     that she's been a problem, but having her here limits my freedom.

     Could you pick her up after lunch on Saturday, April 6?  We're
     planning to leave for Florida on Sunday.

     I'll call you this weekend to confirm.

     Love,



     Rose
```

- Remind the reader that an agreement was made and you expect it to be honored.

- Set a firm date for the changeover and spell out how it is to take place.

Name
Address
City, State Zip

Date

Dear Harry,

Last weekend I spent hours in the basement searching for a box of 45 rpm records. I was amazed at how much junk I've accumulated and how disorganized I am.

I vowed to bring some order into my life, and I'm starting with a major cleanup. That includes disposing of things I don't need or use. I've scheduled a yard sale for the end of the month.

I don't want the furniture you've stored here to be trashed or sold by mistake. Please make arrangements to remove it within the next few weeks. I'd be glad to help with the heavy lifting.

I'll call you in a few days to set a date for the move.

Best,

Jack

• Make it clear that you will no longer be responsible for the stored item.

• The tone of the letter can be friendly *and* assertive.

Name
Address
City, State Zip

Date

Dear Donna and Mark,

I wish we could be together for Christmas. I'm thinking of you and missing you very much.

I hope you like the gifts I've sent. Maybe next month, when we get together, you'll model them for me. For now, I can only imagine how great they'll look on you.

I love you, and I can't wait to see you. Enjoy the holidays, and get ready for some extra hugs when I come out to see you in January.

Love,

Dad

- Separation from loved ones can be painful, especially during family holidays, such as Christmas. A warm letter can help to fill the void.

- Gift-giving is nice, but it's equally important to tell loved ones that they're missed and that you're thinking of them.

Name
Address
City, State Zip

Date

Dear Aunt Edith and Uncle Jack,

This has been an unusual year. Each of us has had to deal with significant change, but it's been 100% positive. For example, the company Scott works for was sold this year. We heard rumors of massive layoffs, and we prepared for the worst. Not only did Scott survive, he received a promotion and a raise!

Both children have moved into apartments with friends. Lee is a copywriter with an advertising agency and Paula has a civilian job at Fort Benning. As for me, I "fell into" a home business. Lee's agency needed outside people to type envelopes, insert brochures, and hand-address special promotions. I volunteered, liked the work, and offered my services to other companies in the area. Would you believe I now have two employees? I may have to rent office space!

We're going to give ourselves another six months, and if things continue to go well, we're going to buy an RV. Scott's always wanted one, and he's promised that our first trip will be to visit you in New Mexico. If that news doesn't scare you off, let us know and we'll make definite plans.

Will you call or write to bring us up-to-date on how retirement is agreeing with you? If I know the two of you, you're up to your eyebrows in all sorts of activities.

Speaking for Scott and the children, have a wonderful Christmas and a happy and healthy New Year.

With love and affection,

Kristin

- Stay positive in holiday updates.

- Make it clear that you want two-way communication. Ask the readers to reciprocate.

Name
Address
City, State Zip

Date

Dear Marlene,

I'm counting the days until Christmas! I've looked forward to your visit all year.

I'll try to balance the usual frantic holiday pace with long stretches of time for conversation and "hanging out." The most important thing is that we'll all be together this year.

Let me know the details of your arrival and length of stay (I hope you'll be with us through New Year's Day!).

Your <u>presence</u> is the best present you could give me.

Love from your baby sister,

Pam

• Remind the reader of their commitment.

• Emphasize how important the visit is to you.

Name
Address
City, State Zip

Date

Dear Dad,

Now that I'm a father, I find I appreciate you more than ever.

Every time I'm about to tell my son I'm too tired to play with him, I do a quick about-face because of the example you set for me. It never occurred to me, until recently, that you might have been tired, or upset, or just wanted to be left alone when you came home from work. But you always had time for me, no matter what.

If I'm a good father—and I think I am—it's because you've been my role model. Thanks for everything, Dad. I'm thinking of you and I love you.

With great affection,

Stuart

• Parents love to hear that you recognize what they've done for you.

• There's no greater compliment than to tell someone they provided a wonderful role model.

Thank You for Everything, Mom (Mother's Day) (4-36)

Name
Address
City, State Zip

Date

Dear Mom,

Being away for Mother's Day makes me feel sad on the one hand, but surprisingly upbeat on the other. I'm sad that I can't be there to give you a hug and a kiss and take you out to dinner. But I'm upbeat because the separation has given me some quiet time to reflect on our relationship.

All through my life, people have remarked on my positive outlook on life...how I look on the bright side, no matter the situation. Guess where that came from? I realize, Mom, that you've given me an attitude—a mind set—that's more valuable than any material reward.

For as long as I can remember, you've made me feel loved and secure, happy and successful, confident and assured. You've always taught me to take responsibility for myself, which has helped me grow and achieve.

I like the woman you shaped. And I love you for all the effort you put into doing it. I may not be with you physically, but I know you can feel my thoughts. I appreciate you and all you've given me. Happy Mother's Day.

Your loving daughter,

Jill

- A personal note is often worth more than the most expensive gift.

- Words that show caring such as "love" and "appreciation" make a parent happy.

Name
Address
City, State Zip

Date

Dear Dad,

Maybe it was the Valentine's Day ads that got to me, but as I started thinking about you a flood of wonderful childhood memories filled my head.

It makes me laugh to think how Mom would roll her eyes when she couldn't tear you away from a game of touch football with the neighborhood kids. You were as much a kid as any of them!

I thought about our family history: the stories you told us about your parents and grandparents, and your struggles to establish yourself and support us. I realized that your history is my history too. And I want Jody and Mark to feel it's their history, so I continue to tell your stories to them.

You're so unique and special, and you always made me feel that way, too. You've given me so much. I hope you know how much I love and appreciate you.

Your loving daughter,

Janice

• This kind of loving letter will be read again and again.

• Try to incorporate shared experiences. It helps set a nostalgic mood.

Valentine Message to Wife (4-38)

Name
Address
City, State Zip

Date

Dear Patty,

Whether you're carting diapers or dressing for dinner, whether you're pulling weeds or just out of the shower, the effect is always the same: You look absolutely wonderful to me.

You're as fresh and fascinating as the day we met. You're more than I ever dreamed possible, and I love you and need you so very much.

Please be my Valentine forever.

Your adoring husband,

Joe

- It's reassuring for the reader to know that you find them as attractive as ever.

- Saying "I love you" is important; saying "I need you" is equally important in some relationships, not so appropriate in others. Choose your words carefully.

Dealing With Banks, Credit, Taxes and Insurance 5

A well thought-out letter to an institution will accomplish four objectives. It will (1) save you time because you won't have to make a personal visit, (2) prevent an unpleasant confrontation if you are emotional about the issue, (3) help you set forth the facts, step-by-step, to get the results you want and (4) put you "on record" if a dispute ever occurs.

A letter to an institution should be different in style from one you write to a relative, friend or close associate. While Aunt Barbara may love reading a long, rambling, free-flowing letter, people at credit agencies, banks and government agencies do not. In fact, a letter that doesn't get to the point quickly may be misinterpreted or—still worse—ignored.

State your objective clearly and succinctly, and offer supporting data. If you sound overwrought, your message may be lost. Write for results, not for reactions.

Banks. Although there have been attempts in recent years to humanize the image that financial institutions present to the public, banks remain largely faceless and mechanical in their dealings with customers. Don't make the mistake of writing as if a caring friend will be reading your missive.

Avoid the temptation to include personal information in your correspondence; it's far more important that you provide the particulars the bank needs in order to respond. And as fine as your writing technique may be, it's no substitute for having complete, accurate records of all transactions at your fingertips, and presenting them plainly when called for.

When you write to a bank, always highlight your account number prominently. And if you expect a response to your correspondence, ask for it. Don't assume it will be sent automatically.

Credit. Problems with credit can haunt your chances to obtain loans, mortgages and credit cards. People often get so upset that they use inflammatory language to deal with credit disputes, when it's level-headed communication that is required to resolve them.

Keep in mind that you're not being singled out for persecution. Mistakes happen within every type of company, and if you're using credit, chances are you'll be the victim of a mistake or two by a credit organization at some point in your life.

As with a bank, clearly list your account number and state the problem or request. If you have supporting documents or evidence of an error, include them with your letter. Always ask for written confirmation of any adjustment or settlement.

Taxes. If you run into problems with taxes, you will have the dubious pleasure of dealing with bureaucratic agencies. If you have to respond to city, state or federal tax offices, your best bet is to work through an experienced CPA. But if you feel you can handle tax-related problems on your own, be certain to stick *only* to the area in dispute.

Identify yourself by your social security or tax ID number, and be certain to retain copies of all correspondence, including any required forms that may accompany your letter.

Insurance. Be specific about the name of the policy, your policy number, and any data that's to be changed, added or deleted when you write to an insurance agent or company. Since discrepancies about coverage may occur only after a tragedy occurs, it's imperative that you understand your coverage, and that your insurer understands your directives. Put your requests and inquiries in writing and ask for written responses so you have proof of each exchange.

I'm Closing My Account because of Poor Service (5-01)

Name
Address
City, State Zip

Date

Mr. Herman Krulisky
President
Bay Area Bank
1188 Praesidio Street
San Francisco, CA 94129

Dear Mr. Krulisky:

You've lost a good customer. I've had my money in Bay Area Bank for twelve years, but I can no longer tolerate the rudeness and poor management.

What's wrong? Here are three examples:

1) At lunchtime on Fridays, the busiest time of the week, there are only two teller windows open and lines stretch to the street.

2) I have waited as long as ten minutes for one of your desk people to finish a personal call before letting me into my safe deposit box.

3) Last month my statement was inaccurate, and when I called to straighten it out, the person I spoke to was rude to the point of blaming me for the bank's mistake.

I have closed my personal checking account, my business account and my Money Market account. I'm switching to a bank where the customer matters.

Sincerely,

Kathryn Bygant

- Get right to the point.

- Be specific about your complaints. Your letter could be an instrument of change that will benefit customers and employees.

Name
Address
City, State Zip

Date

Customer Service Department
Universal Credit
P.O. Box 4558-7390
Boulder, CO 80302   Re: Card #2331 4534 2200

Dear Sir or Madam:

Due to our divorce, effective April 3, 19XX I will not be responsible for any charges made by Mary L. Darnell after that date.

Please issue a new card in my name only, and send it to the above address.

Thank you for your attention to this matter.

Very truly yours,

William P. Darnell

- Be sure to reference your credit card number.

- A simple, straightforward notification is all that's necessary.

I'm Closing My Credit Card Account (5-03)

Name
Address
City, State Zip

Date

Credit Card Department
Midstates Bank
14 Wilmington Boulevard
Wilmington, DE 19899
0401

Re: Acct.# 3009 4214 3200

Dear Sir or Madam:

Please terminate my UNIVERSAL credit card account immediately.

Enclosed are (1) a check for the outstanding balance, and (2) my credit card, which I have cut in half.

The account is in the name of: Paula Berschler Levine
228B Needham Terrace
Claymont, DE 19703

Please send a confirmation that the account has been closed, and a statement reflecting a zero balance.

Thank you for your prompt attention.

Very truly yours,

Paula Berschler Levine

- There's no need for explanation. State what you want done, and give the bank the specific information it needs.

- Ask for a confirmation that your instructions have been followed.

Name
Address
City, State Zip

Date

TRAVELON Bank Card
Credit Department
P.O.Box 1666
Atlanta, GA 30302   Re: Acct.# 4535 2111 3200 3101

Dear Sir or Madam:

I'm a good TRAVELON customer. I've had my card for two years, I use it frequently, and I always pay my bills on time.

Therefore, I'm asking for an increase on my line of credit from $1,500 to $3,000, effective immediately.

Please notify me of your action.

Thank you.

Beverly Staler-Leone

- Briefly mention your good payment history.

- State the amount of credit you're requesting.

Name
Address
City, State Zip

Date

Mr. Walter Chalmers
Customer Service Department
TRAVELON Bank Card
P.O. Box 1666
Atlanta, GA 30302   Re: Acct.# 2121 4767 4100 8432

Dear Mr. Chalmers:

As we discussed yesterday, my TRAVELON credit card was stolen on January 19, 19XX. This letter confirms my request to cancel it immediately, and to have a new one issued.

I understand that I will not be responsible for any charges over $50 made after January 18, 19XX.

Following is the information you will need to cancel the old card and process a new one:

Julia F. Soloway
79 North Valley Road
Wichita, KS 67233

Your quick response will be appreciated.

Very truly yours,

Julia F. Soloway

- State the urgency at the beginning of your letter. Make sure that you say you want a new card issued.

- Restate your understanding of your liability.

Name
Address
City, State Zip

Date

Gibraltar Savings Bank
224 Mountain Boulevard
Boulder, CO 80302   Re: Acct.# SA1111 346 9889 02

Dear Sir or Madam:

Please remove my name as trustee for my son's savings account as of January 25, 19XX. On that date he will turn twenty one, and will be legally responsible for administering his own affairs.

The account is now listed as follows:

Jane Markham Petyk ITF Thomas Petyk

Please confirm the change in writing. The address remains the same. If you have any questions, please telephone me at my office (303) 555-2200.

Thank you.

Very truly yours,

Jane Markham Petyk

• This is a no-frills letter. It simply requires stating your request, and giving the information necessary to make the change.

• Provide your phone number in case the reader has any questions.

Name
Address
City, State Zip

Date

Ms. Erin Reilly
MainTrust Bank
100 Main Street
Covington, KY 41016   Re: Account# LT3540001125

Dear Ms. Reilly:

Confirming our phone conversation today, I was shocked to learn that one of my checks bounced, and I want to know why.

Check number: 2003
Written to: Blue Ridge Electric Company
Amount: $147.35
Dated: March 7, 19XX

My account balance has never dipped below five hundred dollars. Yet this check to my utility company has been returned marked "insufficient funds." They are threatening to turn off my service.

Please do the following to correct your error:

1) Put the check through again.
2) Remove the "insufficient funds" charge from my account.
3) Send me a written explanation of how this error occurred.
4) Send a written explanation and an apology to the Blue Ridge Electric Co.

Very truly yours,

Salvatore Rizzo

- This should be a follow up to a phone call so that you have a record of reque corrections.

- Separate critical information from the body of your letter.

Name
Address
City, State Zip

Date

Billing Supervisor
Burkett's Department Stores
One Riverside Plaza   Re: Account# 72-332069

Dear Sir or Madam:

My current bill, dated 4/22, is incorrect. It indicates that I purchased a pair of jeans for $49.95 at your Honolulu store. I've
never purchased jeans from any of your stores. In fact, I've never
been in the Honolulu store.

Please correct your records, and send a confirmation that my
account has been properly credited. I'd appreciate your prompt
attention.

Sincerely,

George Haleawa

Reference your account number to ensure that you are credited properly.

There's no need to be antagonistic. The vast majority of credit disputes are resolved
amicably and quickly.

DEALING WITH BANKS, CREDIT, TAXES AND INSURANCE

Name
Address
City, State Zip

Date

Four Star DiningCard
P.O. Box 4444-090
Wilmington, DE 19850   Re: Account# 2207657-12

Dear Sir or Madam:

There's an error on my monthly statement, and I'd like it corrected immediately.

I've been charged $130.00 for a meal at Le Petit Jardin in Santa Fe, New Mexico on January 23. That charge is incorrect because:

1) I've never been to Santa Fe.
2) On January 23 I was in the hospital undergoing surgery (attached is a copy of my hospital bill.)
3) My credit card has never left my possession.

Please remove this charge from my bill.

Thank you.

Very truly yours,

Amelia de Long

- State your reasons for believing that the creditor is in error, and supply proof, if possible.

- Request that the charge be removed from your statement.

You Didn't Credit My Payment (5-10)

Name
Address
City, State Zip

Date

Accounts Receivable Manager
Clearway Cable Company
1424 Republic Avenue
Topeka, KS 66677   Re: Account# 28781A

Dear Sir or Madam:

I'm up-to-date on my payments, but I'm not being credited for them. Here is the chronology of events that will help you get my account current:

1. As part of a neighborhood protest for poor service, I paid half of my November and December bills (check #s 3965 and 3944 for $28.25 each).

2. Service problems were corrected in late December, so I sent the withheld balance (check #4009 for $56.50).

3. In January, I received a letter threatening to cut off my service. I ignored it, since I had made good on the deferred payments, and sent in my monthly payment (check #4020 for $56.50).

4. In February, I received another threatening letter, this time telling me I was two months in arrears. I decided it was time to write before things got out of hand.

Copies of cancelled checks, corresponding to the list above, are enclosed. If any questions remain, you can reach me by day at (913) 555-3387.

Sincerely,

Allen Milton

• Don't be emotional. Just supply pertinent facts.

• Simplicity counts when trying to resolve payment problems. Using numbered lists presents information clearly.

Name
Address
City, State Zip

Date

Northwest Electric Company
40 Tacoma Boulevard
Tacoma, WA 96439   Re: Account# 33807

Dear Sir or Madam:

I realize my account is in arrears, and I'm committed to bringing it up to date.

Your records will show that I've always paid my bills on time. But a recent illness has made it difficult for me to meet my financial obligations.

Now I'm working again, and I want to pay off my overdue electric bill as quickly as I can. I'd appreciate your cooperation.

Would this be agreeable? I'll pay each month's bill in full, and add $20 towards the overdue portion each month until the entire amount ($287) is paid off.

May I count on Northwest Electric Company to keep me out of the dark?

Very truly yours,

Sharon McOscar

- Briefly explain that recent hardship has temporarily disrupted your good credit history.

- Offer a reasonable way to resolve your debt.

Name
Address
City, State Zip

Date

Mr. Harold Albritton
Credit Manager
Buckley's Department Store
211 Monroe Mall
Norwood, OH 45212

Dear Mr. Albritton:

I won't respond to future collection letters; my attorney will.

I've called your credit department three times to discuss your billing error. Each time, a very pleasant—but apparently incompetent—person agreed that that the error was the store's, and would be corrected. Shortly after each call, I received a nasty collection letter.

I've enclosed copies of your letters, my telephone log with the dates of my calls and the name of the person with whom I spoke, a cancelled check showing that the bill was paid, and my cut-up Buckley's credit card.

I'll consider any subsequent collection letters as harassment, and I'll instruct my attorney to file a very public suit against you and your company.

Sincerely,

Sarah Trewell

- When all else fails, take the offensive. Most companies will go to great lengths to avoid bad publicity.

- Carefully document your position.

Correct the Error on My Credit Report (5-13)

Name
Address
City, State Zip

Date

Access Credit Reporting System
2446 Main Street
Newark, NJ 07102   Re: Report #345870912

Dear Sir or Madam:

There is an error on my credit report which needs to be corrected.

The report shows an outstanding balance of $234.75 owed to Collier's Department Store. This balance was paid in full on May 16, 19XX. Attached is a copy of the canceled check.

Please do the following:

1) Remove the outstanding balance.
2) Send me a copy of the corrected report.

Thank you.

Very truly yours,

Joseph A. Radvansky

• Provide proof such as a canceled check, receipt, letter, etc. that the outstanding debt has been paid.

• Request a copy of the corrected report.

Send Me a Copy of My Credit Report (5-14)

Name
Address
City, State Zip

Date

Access Credit Reporting System
2446 Main Street
Newark, NJ 07012

Dear Sir or Madam:

Please send me a copy of my credit report. My address is noted above, and my Social Security number is 122-09-3551.

Thank you.

Very truly yours,

Marian B. Kidder

- Be sure to include your Social Security number when requesting a credit report.

- Keep your request simple. There's no need to give details of why you're making the request.

Name
Address
City, State Zip

Date

POWERBASE Credit Corporation
P.O. Box 1000
Dallas, TX 75260

Dear Sir or Madam:

Why have you refused my request for a POWERBASE credit card?

I'm a homeowner, I'm gainfully employed, and I have an excellent credit rating. If I'm not the ideal credit risk, who is?

Please send me an explanation. Better yet—why don't you review your decision and send me a credit card.

Very truly yours,

Daphne Dahlberg

- Make your case as a good candidate for credit.

- Request an explanation for why your credit application was turned down.

Name
Address
City, State Zip

Date

Internal Revenue Service
Holtsville, NY 00501

RE: Norman and Page Weller
SS# 160-55-3110 and 095-60-1683
Disallowance of Deduction on Form 1040 (19XX)

To Whom It May Concern:

Your disallowance of our $4,000 deduction for IRA contributions is an error. On the notice you sent, you indicated the reason for the disallowance is that one of us is covered by a retirement plan.

As you can tell from the enclosed copies of our W-2 forms for 19XX, this is incorrect. Neither of the forms is checked in the pension plan block.

Since neither of us was covered by a retirement plan in 19XX, we request that you correct your records to (1) allow the IRA deduction, and (2) abate the tax and penalty we were assessed.

Very truly yours,

Norman Weller

- The IRS makes errors, as does any organization. Contrary to public opinion, they also rectify their errors.

- State your case, supported by facts, and don't allow emotions to intrude. End by asking for a correction.

Name
Address
City, State Zip

Date

Internal Revenue Service
Treasury Department
Washington, D.C. 20224   Re: Underpayment of refund
                                SS# 122-98-5462

Dear Sir or Madam:

I believe the refund check you sent me was incorrect.

According to my completed 19XX tax return, I am entitled to a
refund of $1,287.65. Yet you sent me a check for $128.76, with
no explanation regarding the discrepancy.

It appears that the amount due was incorrectly keypunched into
your computer.

Please correct and acknowledge the error, and send me a check
for the additional $1,158.89.

Very truly yours,

Bonnie Louise Pevaroff

- Reference your social security number to identify yourself.

- Clearly state the discrepancy and request that it be rectified. Also request a written
  acknowledgement of error on the part of the IRS.

Name
Address
City, State Zip

Date

Internal Revenue Service   Re: Overpayment of Refund
Philadelphia, PA 19147   SS# 141-48-0064

Dear Sir or Madam:

I was scheduled to receive a refund check of $1,142.67, but received a check for $3,478.00. I've enclosed a check for $2,335.33, which is the amount of overpayment you erroneously made. I trust this will close the matter.

Very truly yours,

Julio Gonzalez

- When the IRS makes an overpayment, problems may follow unless you immediately send a letter with a check in the amount of the overpayment. Send it return receipt requested.

- According to one CPA firm, the IRS has been known to penalize people who have received overpayments, even though they *verbally* reported the error.

Name
Address
City, State Zip

Date

Internal Revenue Service
Chicago, IL 60604   Re: Resubmission of Form 1099

Dear Sir or Madam:

I filed my taxes with an incorrect Social Security number, so I've enclosed a new Form 1099, with the correct social security number.

Incorrect Number: 155-09-8735
Correct Number: 155-09-8753

I apologize for the error. If there are any questions, please contact me at (312) 555-4943.

Sincerely,

Jack Jerome

- If you file your return with an incorrect social security number, it's recommended that you refile a new return. Trying to correct the original error is often an exercise in futility.

- The new submission will be entered properly in the IRS computers, which will negate any problems that may arise due to the original filing.

Name
Address
City, State Zip

Date

Ms. Maria Soldano
Audit Adjustment Branch
New Jersey Dept. of Taxation   Re: Cary Lockhart
Trenton, NJ 08646   SS# 151-35-7007

Dear Ms. Soldano:

Here are our answers to your three primary questions:
1. I haven't been able to locate my cancelled checks from 1992. I'm still looking, and I'll be back to you within a week.

2. The $32,000 in tax payments/prior year credit on line 31 of our 1992 tax return was paid/credited as follows:

Credit from 1991 return	$ 4,197
Paid on or about 12/31/92	17,803
Paid on or about 4/15/93	<u>10,000</u>
Total line 31	$32,000

3. I have no record of ever receiving the $4,756 refund or credit indicated on Form NJ-601, Notice of Adjustment, dated June 13, 1996. Therefore, it has not been applied as a credit.

I hope this resolves matters. However, if you need additional information, please call me during the day at (908) 555-3882.

Sincerely,

Cary Lockhart

• It is strongly recommended that a tax professional be engaged to handle audit inquiries and responses.

• Stick to the facts. Respond only to specific questions.

Name
Address
City, State Zip

Date

Ms. Alice Long
Waverly Hall Insurance
1910 Beacon Street   Re: Change of Beneficiary
Stone Mountain, GA 30087   Life Insurance Policy# 0073A22A

Dear Ms. Long:

My wife, Georgia, passed away nearly a month ago. I'd like to continue to carry my policy, but substitute co-beneficiaries, as follows:

    Arlene Claire Gorham Ross (my daughter)
    Harvey Edward Gorham (my son)

If any forms need to be signed, please send them to the address shown above. If any questions need to be answered, you can reach me at (404) 555-6693.

I'd appreciate your prompt acknowledgement and processing of this request.

Very truly yours,

Sherman Gorham

- The more key information you provide—clearly formatted—the faster the transition is likely to take place.

- Never assume that a request has been honored. Ask for an acknowledgement, and if it's not received in an acceptable amount of time, follow up.

Name
Address
City, State Zip

Date

Mr. Bradley Mortensen
Flemington Insurance Brokers
599 Powhatan Trail   Re: Homeowner's Policy
Thibodaux, LA 70310   #125-32-771B-363

Dear Brad:

I was one of the lucky ones when a twister visited my neighborhood last week. But I may not be so lucky next time.

I pulled out my homeowner's policy to check my coverage on
storm damage, but I'm still not sure what's covered. Would you
please give me a <u>written</u> summary, in everyday English, of what—
if anything—I need to do to protect my investment in my home and
grounds.

May I hear from you within the next couple of weeks?

Sincerely,

Ben Verna

- Insist on a written answer; it may be of value in a dispute.

- Ask for a response within a reasonable time period.

Name
Address
City, State Zip

Ms. Amelia Smith
Taggert Insurance Agency
621 Marigold Drive
Santa Barbara, CA 93160   Re: Policy# VI 277700546

Dear Ms. Smith:

I recently inherited a diamond ring from my grandmother's estate
and I would like to insure it. I have enclosed a copy of the
appraisal and a photograph of the ring.

Please confirm, in writing, that you have added the ring to my
valuable items policy. Also advise me how the addition will affect
my premium payments.

Thank you.

Sincerely,

Rosemary Rohner

- Attach a copy of the appraisal.

- Ask for written confirmation that your instructions have been followed.

Name
Address
City, State Zip

Date

Ms. Marika Alexis
Quick Claim Casualty Company
42 W. 19th Street
Enid, OK 73701   Re: Policy# 520AZ-19930

Dear Marika:

As you requested, here are the details on our new car:

Make: Ford
Year: 1995
Model: SE Coupe
VIN: HAC58F6E5K812663
Air Bag: Yes/Driver's Side
Anti-theft Device: Yes

I'm the primary driver and, as with our last car, it will be used to go to and from work each day (a round-trip commute of 20 miles). All coverage and deductibles will remain as before.

Thanks for your help, Marika. As always, it's a pleasure to work with you.

Sincerely,

Wesley Greycloud

• Although most insurers cover you from the moment you call, it's important to put the information in writing.

• This information is best faxed or sent via certified mail.

Name
Address
City, State Zip

Date

Mr. Garson James
Brookfield/Silver Insurance
371 Pacific Street   Re: Homeowner's Policy
Hartford, CT 06103   #54-65-3112-7

Dear Garson:

When I heard how much my neighbor sold his home for, alarms
went off in my head. It made me realize that my home is seriously
under-insured.

Effective immediately, please upgrade my Homeowner's coverage
as follows:

Dwelling:	$250,000
Personal Property:	$175,000
Personal Liability:	$500,000

Would you please acknowledge that the change has been made?
I don't want to wait for your invoice to be certain I'm covered at
the new levels. Thanks.

Sincerely,

Steven Margolis

• Indentations highlight key information.

• Ask for an acknowledgement. Don't assume anything.

Name
Address
City, State Zip

Date

Mr. Kent Broussard
Global Insurance Agency
2412 W. Park Place
Fairfield, CT 06430

Dear Kent:

I suppose it was the latest rate increase that forced me to do some comparison shopping, and I don't like what I've learned. It appears that at least three other insurance companies charge less than the one your firm recommended for exactly the same automobile coverage.

If you want to retain my business, please call to explain why I'm paying so much.

Sincerely,

Linda Sue Chaplin

- By making it clear that they are about to lose your business, you can force your agent to respond promptly.

- State that you're willing to listen (otherwise you might not get a response). Chances are the agent will come up with some ideas that will lower your premium.

Employment 6

Letters that deal with employment situations should be thought of as sales letters, not self-disclosure letters. They are meant to exhibit your best traits and appeal to the needs of the reader (the prospective employer). Whether seeking a job or resigning from one, you want the reader to think of you positively. And the way to do that is to enthusiastically accentuate your assets.

Job search. A cover letter for a resume, a request for an interview, or correspondence with a prospective employer should be written not from your perspective, but from the perspective of the reader. It's not what *you* find interesting, motivating and impressive that counts; it's what the prospective employer might find of value that's important. An employer won't meet with you just because you want a job, but they will interview you because you have specific skills to offer their organization. If you take the time to learn about (1) the organization and its position in the marketplace, and (2) the reader's interests and needs, you'll be more successful in your job search.

Prospective employers give high points to people who take time to do their homework prior to being interviewed. In addition, arming yourself with as much information as possible will allow you to be relaxed and to give the best interview you're capable of.

Resignations. No matter what the reason for leaving your current position may be, you'll do yourself—and possibly your future employment—a great disservice if the departure isn't handled with dignity and thought.

Your resignation letter leaves your employer with a final impression, and it should summon good feelings, rather than stirring up memories of past slights or disagreements. It provides an opportunity to say thank you for your employment, and it's an inexpensive insurance policy for the day when a prospective future employer calls your company for a reference.

Also, keep in mind that situations change. Someday you may want to return to a former employer, and it will be much easier if you're remembered as a positive and appreciative person.

Name
Address
City, State Zip

Date

Mr. Harry Needham
Current Concepts, Inc.
50 North Madison Street
Madison, WI 53777

Dear Harry:

When you hired me, I thought I had a lot to offer...but I didn't know how much I had to learn. Now, as I take inventory of the skills, insight and understanding I'm bringing to my new job, I realize how far you've brought me.

It's ironic that I'm thanking you for giving me so much, since I've used it as a springboard to another position. I feel somewhat guilty for leaving, but I also feel pleased to have the chance to apply your management practices and principles elsewhere.

I don't know how to repay you, Harry, except to promise that I'll continue what you started. Now I can do for others what you did for me: turn the work place into a stimulating environment... a place of challenge, opportunity and growth.

Thank you so much for helping to turn me into the businessperson I've become. I hope we stay in touch.

With great admiration,

Dennis Solomon

- If someone helped you achieve your potential, be certain to acknowledge their role.

- An ex-boss can become a boss again, or a very valuable resource. Use every opportunity to cement relationships.

Name
Address
City, State Zip

Date

Mr. Mark Hoppen
Automated Work Force
Robbins Avenue at Pratt Street
Whittier, CA 90610

Dear Mark:

So far, my new job is everything I hoped it would be. I like the pace, the no-nonsense approach to forecasting, and even the demands it makes on me. This management group asks a lot, but they give you the tools you need.

I'd like to tell you more (I know you'll get a kick out of their unique perspective on customer service), so let's get together for lunch some day soon. We worked together for so long, I don't want to lose touch. Will you call me at 555-1300? I'd like to hear from you.

Kindest regards,

Art

- If you would like a work-related friendship to continue after your departure, say so. The person "left behind" may need reassurance.

- Indicate that you still have some interests in common.

Name
Address
City, State Zip

Date

Dear Bern,

I'm going through one of those periods in life when I wish someone would just grab me by the lapels, shake me, and tell me what
to do. Since I respect your opinion very much, perhaps I can
impose on you to help snap me out of my indecision.

Here's the situation: About six months ago, I took a sales job with
a North Carolina-based company. I was assured that I could
operate from Minneapolis where, as you know, I have family,
friends and home. All of a sudden I started getting pressure to
relocate to North Carolina. Management has decided that I have
a lot to offer, and they want me to work more closely with them.
This is a first step, I'm told, to moving into management.

While I'm flattered by the attention, I'm not sure I'm ready to alter
my life so radically just now. It's taken me 38 years to reach a
point where I'm doing what I want to do, and the thought of
change has me frozen.

You know me as well as anyone. Will you give my situation some
thought, and then call me at 612-555-4480? I'll fill you in on the
specifics when we talk, but this will give you a headstart. You're
so good at examining all sides of a question, I can't wait to hear
from you.

Your friend,

Max

- Don't beat around the bush; if you want advice, ask for it.

- Highlight the dilemma in broad terms; save details for a more in-depth discussion.

Name
Address
City, State Zip

Date

Mr. Lawrence Kingman
Sales Manager
Gross Enterprises
5800 West Ferndale Industrial Park
Delaware City, DE 19706

Dear Mr. Kingman:

If you're like most successful sales managers, you're never
satisfied with your company's sales. An extra push here, an
additional call there, and your team could generate an additional
ten percent.

Well, I'm the person who can supply that extra ten—or fifteen, or
even twenty—percent. I've consistently set territory records at my
current company...and I'd like the opportunity to do the same for
you.

I'll explain why I want to work for your company when we meet.
And I'll show you how you can put my successful experience to
work for your future growth.

I'll call you next Wednesday at 10:00 a.m. to arrange an appointment. If you won't be available, please contact me at (302) 555-
1886, or leave word when it would be convenient for us to talk.

Very truly yours,

Franklin Robbins

- To get an interview, you must convince your "target" that you can achieve something
  that they need. Increased sales, more productivity, lower costs, etc.

- By being specific about the time of a call, you're more likely to make contact.

Request for Interview, Follow-Up to Ad (6-05)

Name
Address
City, State Zip

Date

Human Resources Department
Pace, Barten & Denker
Woodley Center/Suite 200   Re: Executive Secretary Position
Danbury, CT 06813   Advertised 6/23, Danbury Gazette

Dear Sir or Madam:

I've served as the "right arm" for senior executives for nearly twenty years. Although I don't have the associate degree you request, I think you'll find that my secretarial and office management skills (not to mention English and grammar skills) are superior.

I'm proficient in word processing (WordPerfect), spreadsheets (Lotus 1 2 3) and databases (Paradox). Since I'm from the "old school," I'm also proficient in shorthand and dictaphone transcription.

When we have the opportunity to meet, I'll elaborate on my work experience—which seems to complement your needs—and supply you with strong references. I can be reached during the day at (203) 555-1818, or in the evening at (203) 555-5067.

I'm looking forward to discussing the position with you.

Very truly yours,

Christine Alcindor

• Show how your skills or experience match the requirements listed in the ad.

• Be sure to identify the ad and the newspaper, otherwise your letter may not get to the right party.

Request for Interview, Follow-Up to Phone Call (6-06)

Name
Address
City, State Zip

Date

Ms. Lenore Cullen
Worldwide Fashions, Inc.
1377 Gilbert Avenue
New York, NY 10016

Dear Ms. Cullen:

After thinking about our phone conversation, I believe I have a lot
to offer Worldwide Fashions. I've enclosed the resume you
requested, with the reminder that it presents only a partial picture.
By granting me an interview, you'll have the opportunity to see the
full range of my work and my solutions to a number of design
challenges.

Thanks for spending so much time on the phone with me. I'll call
within a week to arrange a meeting date.

Sincerely,

Suzette Frankel

• Don't just say that you want a meeting; explain why it will be beneficial to the prospective interviewer.

• Take the initiative by saying that you'll do the phone follow-up to arrange the interview.

Name
Address
City, State Zip

Date

Mr. Leslie Whittaker
Creative Services Manager
Lakeside Plastics
5700 E. Melrose Boulevard
Roselle, IL 60172

Dear Mr. Whittaker:

Roger Neilson, in your manufacturing group, suggested that I contact you about the opening for a writer on the company newsletter.

One of the things Roger felt would be of great value to your company is my versatility; I can fill many roles. For example, I've been a reporter (Maplewood Community News), an advertising copywriter (The Tricewell Agency), and an editor (The Daily Report). That means that you have the flexibility to use my skills in multiple functions.

Roger said that he'd be happy to fill you in on why he feels I'd be an asset to your operation (you can reach him at Ext. 211). I hope you'll take him up on his offer. And I'd like to have the opportunity to meet you and present my credentials in person. I'll call you next week to set up an appointment.

Cordially,

Richard Fujioka

- If an employee will give you an endorsement, it represents an excellent "leg up" on your competition.

- Remember: Your goal is to get an interview. Don't overload your letter with data.

Name
Address
City, State Zip

Date

Mr. Julian Kasten
Arrow Executive Search, Inc.
48 W. Saturn Avenue
Charlotte, NC 28276

Dear Mr. Kasten:

Every book I've read says you don't contact executive recruiters; they contact you. But my guess is you'll overlook protocol if the talent is highly marketable. And I am.

I'm skilled at putting ideas into action. In fact, I have 12 years of consistently high quality problem-solving and profit-producing achievements behind me...with the promise of many more successful years to come.

The enclosed resume will give you some idea of what I've done and for whom. A personal interview will help convince you that I can be a valuable addition to your executive bank.

I'll call within the week to arrange an interview.

Sincerely,

Victor Brodie

• George Bernard Shaw wrote that people who get on in the world are those "who get up and look for the circumstances they want, and if they can't find them, make them." This writer accomplishes that with this letter.

• Indicate that you will pursue the interview with a phone call, and be sure that you do.

Name
Address
City, State Zip

Date

Mr. Tyrone Jackson
Farragut Industries
832 Tacony Street
Youngstown, OH 44537

Dear Mr. Jackson:

Although you indicated you had more interviews to conduct before making a final decision, I want you to know how interested I am in the controller's position.

You made it clear that you're looking for someone who is every bit as good a manager as he is a creative financial planner. When you combine my accomplishments in management accounting with my industry-specific background, I think you'll find that I fit your profile perfectly.

Thank you for an excellent interview and the opportunity to gain some insight into an outstanding organization. I hope we have the chance to talk again.

Very truly yours,

Ronald Chessy

• Enthusiasm sells. If you feel an interview went well, let the interviewer know it. It will mark you as someone who is in tune with others' feelings (a people person).

• Take the opportunity to reiterate how your abilities mesh with the job description.

Name
Address
City, State Zip

Date

Mr. George Yates
Griffith Industries
1400 Randall Street West
Sioux City, IA 51161

Dear Mr. Yates:

I may not have gotten the job at Griffith, but I received a terrific education. I can't thank you enough for your time, effort and interest.

Armed with the feedback from my interviews, I'll work on the areas in which you feel I'm weak...and I'll polish the strong points, too. I was so impressed with you and Griffith Industries that I hope I'll have the opportunity to reapply in the future. I plan to be prepared when I do!

Thank you. I have a feeling we'll meet again.

Sincerely,

Steven Oates

- Always acknowledge an interview, win or lose. It marks you as someone with class and savvy.

- Let the interviewer know that you understand and appreciate the effort that they put into the meeting(s).

Name
Address
City, State Zip

Date

Mr. Taylor Caldwell
Universal Garden Equipment
996 Gateway Boulevard
St. Louis, MO 63103

Dear Mr. Caldwell:

I appreciate the job offer. In fact, I'm flattered that you made me your first choice out of so many candidates. But I'm going to need a few days to think about it before making a commitment. Are you willing to wait for an answer until next Monday morning?

This slight delay has nothing to do with your offer or the position; both are outstanding. But there are family matters that must first be resolved, so that if I say "yes," it will be wholeheartedly.

I hope you can wait for my decision, particularly since your organization and the responsibilities you've outlined are so attractive. Unless I hear otherwise from you, I'll call you Monday morning at 9:00 a.m. sharp.

Thanks for the opportunity.

Sincerely,

Gerald Wilkins

• This letter is appropriate only if you were the pursued, rather than the pursuer.

• Don't leave the letter open-ended. Guarantee an answer by a specific time.

Name
Address
City, State Zip

Date

Mr. Adam Dorsey
Dorsey Advertising
13 Walker Park Boulevard
Honolulu, HI 96827

Dear Mr. Dorsey:

I'm flattered that you offered me the position as account supervisor on the Greenlea Pharmaceutical account. It's a prestigious position, and probably the answer to many an adperson's prayer. At this stage in my life, however, I'm not convinced that I'm ready to make the transition from publishing to advertising.

I appreciate the time you, your staff, and your executive recruiter gave me. I can't think of a group that I'd rather work with. But the attraction of my current position pulls hard. Leaving now would make me feel as if I were turning my back on unfinished business, from the company's as well as my own viewpoint.

Thanks again for the opportunity. I wish you much continued success. I hope we cross paths again in the future.

Very truly yours,

Linda Haller

• Deal with positives even in a refusal letter; you never know when you might meet this person sometime in the future.

• Loyalty is a valued trait, even when it's the reason for your not accepting the position.

Name
Address
City, State Zip

Date

Mr. Caleb Berg
Deluxe Packaging Inc.
411 Hamilton Street
Paterson, NJ 07509

Dear Mr. Berg:

Your patience and understanding during the past several months have meant so much to me and my family. Thanks for adjusting my schedule to accommodate my trips to the doctor.

The news from the most recent round of tests is not good. I have a form of chronic leukemia which will require intensive treatment, and months of bed rest. The prognosis for recovery is uncertain.

It's very painful for me to have to say good-bye to my friends at Deluxe Packaging, but my illness leaves me no choice but to resign, effective immediately.

Thank you, Mr. Berg, for being a wonderful supervisor. I'll keep fond memories of my thirteen happy years at Deluxe.

Sincerely,

Ethel White

- Let the reader know that their efforts to accommodate you have not gone unnoticed.

- Make it clear that you have no alternative but to resign, and express regret that this is your only option.

Name
Address
City, State Zip

Date

Mr. Ian Maplewood
Southern Transportation Services
7700 Forsythe Avenue
Jackson, MS 39201

Dear Ian:

It is with great regret that I have to offer my resignation. My husband has received an offer to head the division of his company that's based in Northern Maryland. He and I agree that when something this good comes along for either of us, there's little choice but to take it, even if it disrupts the other's career.

I have so much to do to prepare for the move, I'd appreciate being relieved of my duties as soon as possible. But I'm willing to stay for up to three weeks if you need me.

It's been a pleasure working for you, Ian. You're a unique individual, and your insight, intelligence, and managerial style have helped me to grow personally and professionally. I hope we stay in touch.

Best wishes, and thanks for your friendship and support.

Sincerely,

Sandra Surrey

• Explain that the resignation was based on your spouse's having to move. (It eases the sting.)

• Since you'll be leaving, you may feel comfortable expressing sentiments that you previously left unsaid.

Name
Address
City, State Zip

Date

Ms. Gale Heinbaugh
Abercrombie Advertising, Inc.
4 Derby Court
Louisville, KY 40231

Dear Gale:

The years I've spent producing commercials at Abercrombie have been rewarding and challenging. But motherhood is proving to be rewarding and challenging, too.

I miss my baby when I'm at work. I find myself losing concentration. Giving less than 100%—at work or at home—is not in my nature. So, rather than turn out work that's below my standards, I feel I have to resign. This has not been an easy decision.

Advertising will always be a great love of mine. No doubt, when I no longer have little ones at home, I'll be contacting you again, storyboards and portfolio in hand. I hope you'll welcome me back.

It's been a joy working for you and with you.

Sincerely,

Gaby Pena-Dresher

- Make it clear that you made this decision based on what's best for you *and* for the company. It's in keeping with the loyal, valued professional that you are.

- Let the reader know that this isn't a permanent career decision, and that you'd like to be considered for opportunities in the future.

Name
Address
City, State Zip

Date

Ms. Ellen Bradshaw
Robertson Container Corp.
5104 Ninth Street
St. Paul, MN 55101

Dear Ellen:

I wish I could pick this company up and put it back down someplace in the Phoenix, Arizona area. Since I can't, I have no choice but to offer my resignation.

As you know, my wife's family is concentrated in Arizona. That's one reason for the move. We both feel very strongly about the kids having family around them during their formative years, and we have no family here. Another reason for moving is the positive effect the doctor tells me the heat will have on my cranky, football-scarred knees. He says I'll finally feel <u>my</u> age...not my grandfather's!

Thank you for six wonderful years. I appreciate the guidance you've provided, your faith in my ability, and the many kindnesses you extended to me and my family. I can't tell you how much I've enjoyed working for you, and for Robertson Container. It will be very difficult to leave a work environment that can't be duplicated anywhere else.

We plan to leave in 30 days, Ellen, but I could give you an extra week or so if you need the time to ease the transition. I'll do whatever will help.

Sincerely,

Dick Peoples

- Avoid a lengthy preamble. State your plans up front.

- Take the time to detail the plusses of the current job; a positive recommendation from your employer will be of value in the future.

Name
Address
City, State Zip

Date

Mr. William E. Blenheim
Martin Main Instruments, Inc.
6322 Production Park
St. Louis, MO 63103

Dear Will:

It's reached a point where what's going on outside my office window is more important to me than what's going on inside the office. So to be fair to both of us, I'm offering my resignation.

Because my retirement is a relaxed decision for me, I can work around your schedule. I'm willing to stay on to help you train a replacement (and do whatever else you feel is necessary to ease the transition), but by early Spring, Millie and I plan to start traveling in earnest.

If I can be of future help on any special projects or collaboration, I hope you'll call. I think you'll agree that my instincts and analytical skills are as sharp as ever—only my desire to work full-time has diminished!

Thanks for everything, Will. Let's get together to work out a non-disruptive departure schedule.

Sincerely,

Joe Florentine

- If you have a high-level position, it's a courtesy to give as much time as possible to create an orderly transition.

- If you're willing to consult in the future, be sure to make the company aware of it. Don't assume they'll call unless you invite them to.

Expressing Opinions 7

When you believe strongly in an issue, it's natural to want others to share your view. Persuasion is the art of swaying others to your vision, and persuasion requires tact and the marshalling of facts.

You may wish to express your opinion to a public official, newspaper or a hero of yours. Prepare your letter with the same care you would give a letter to a prospective employer or the object of your affection, even though you're writing to someone you may never meet. The more coherent and convincing your letter, the better its chances of making your point.

Be clear that what you're saying is your opinion (I think, I feel), if that's what it is. Or, if you're stating something as fact, be able to back it up with supporting data.

Getting it off your chest. While it might satisfy your urge to "get even" by throwing an epithet or two at someone who is irritating you, it's far more constructive to state your disapproval or disagreement reasonably and admit that there may be other viewpoints. Then you can suggest the actions you feel should be taken.

Often it helps to spread a little honey at the start of the letter to get the reader on your side, then lead into the criticism or suggested change. Remind the reader that they stand to gain something from paying attention to you. Pressure is fine; abuse isn't.

When expressing an opinion, build credibility and trust by identifying your sources (newspaper article, reference book, tv documentary, etc.) and explaining your logic.

If the idea behind your letter is to simply make a statement and "speak your peace," that's fine. But if you want a response or an action, be sure to ask for one.

Fan letters. Mark Twain once said, "I can live for two months on a good compliment." He probably echoed the feelings of most people, whether they're in the public eye or not.

It's thoughtful to offer letters of praise for outstanding work, as well as for great performances. Rock stars and athletes aren't the only ones deserving of our admiration. A teacher or mentor can be a hero, too.

There are no hard and fast rules when it comes to writing a fan letter—which is really a letter of appreciation—but your best chance of having yours read is to keep it short and simple. Any accompanying requests (e.g., photo, autograph) should be reasonable.

Recipients of fan mail will be most likely to respond to your letter if it seems well thought out and heartfelt. Obsessive, overly doting letters are considered juvenile and may even be thought of as threatening.

Letter to the Editor Requesting Correction (7-01)

Name
Address
City, State Zip

Date

Editor
Morning Call Gazette
1 Paley Plaza
Des Moines, IA 50322

Dear Sir or Madam:

Would you please print a correction in your paper. On December 3, you ran a story on page two, in the metro section of the Morning Call Gazette. The headline was, "Local Woman Wins Award." You listed me, Marion Elderson, as the recipient of the award. I presented the award. The correct name of the recipient is Alma Norris.

Despite the mix-up, we're pleased that you covered our event! Thank you.

Sincerely,

Marion (Mrs.Robert) Elderson

• Be specific about the date the story was published, and its location in the paper.

• Describe what the story said, then what it *should* have said.

Letter to the Editor Regarding New Shopping Mall (7-02)

Name
Address
City, State Zip

Date

Ms. Pearl Sangree
Editor
Baton Rouge Times
1000 Landmark Avenue
Baton Rouge, LA 70621

Dear Ms. Sangree:

I'm concerned about plans to build a shopping mall in the vicinity of the Boynton Middle School for two reasons:

1) A mall will hasten the demise of the economy of our Main Street shopping area.

2) Malls are magnets to young people—for all the wrong reasons. From all I've read, teenagers use the malls as hangouts and for buying and selling drugs, as well as committing other crimes.

I have two children who are students at Boynton. Although they're responsible kids, they are not impervious to peer pressure. I hope I won't have to keep them from becoming involved in the mall "scene."

We don't need another mall. Let's try to find a more positive use for the North Street property.

Sincerely,

Agatha White

- State your opinion or grievance clearly.

- Have a sound basis for your position.

Letter to City Councilperson Regarding Proposed Bill (7-03)

Name
Address
City, State Zip

Date

The Honorable Laughton Charles
City Council
Philadelphia, PA 19107   Re: New Stadium Bill

Dear Sir:

Published reports suggest that you are planning to support a bill to construct a new baseball stadium. I'm a sports fan, Mr. Charles, but I can't see sinking $75 million into a new stadium...particularly since it would require just $3-$5 million to bring our existing stadium up to code.

We live in a city overrun with homeless people, addiction-fueled criminals, dilapidated neighborhoods, racial hostility, and, to add to the overall discomfort, cracked sidewalks and potholed streets. There's no way you can justify spending $75 million to make millionaire athletes and fat-cat corporate types more comfortable!

If you vote "yes," I'll be in the forefront of a movement to see that you're not re-elected.

Very truly yours,

Angel Gonzalez

- The way to stave off an unfavorable vote is to get to a politician *before* the vote. Your opinion isn't worth much after the fact.

- Nonviolent threats are effective tools for swaying votes.

Name
Address
City, State Zip

Date

The Honorable Lucinda Blankenship
Mayor of Montpelier
City Hall
Montpelier, VT 05602

Dear Mayor Blankenship:

Baldridge House and Morris Manor represent Vermont history and tradition, but they've been allowed to fall into disrepair. If city government can find funds to "beautify" hundreds of sterile municipal offices, it should also be able to afford a few gallons of paint to spruce up a piece of our rich heritage.

You ran on a ticket of preserving values. Here's an excellent opportunity for you to make good on your pledge to uphold them. These wonderful homes represent a link with our past. I expect you to lead a fight to maintain that link.

May I know how you stand on this issue?

Very truly yours,

Lauren Foster

- Politicians need to be held accountable for their promises. Writing letters is a primary means of pressuring government officials.

- If you don't ask for an answer, you probably won't get one.

Name
Address
City, State Zip

Date

Dr. Carolyn Larken
Middletown Board of Education
3219 Fellowship Road
Little Rock, AR 72279

Dear Dr. Larken:

From everything I've read, your attempts at diplomacy have been interpreted by a small group of zealots as a "green light" to continue their attack on freedom of thought.

History books are full of examples of how poorly appeasement works as a mediation tool. Every retreat you make emboldens and strengthens the book-burners...and confuses the fence-sitters who mistake the silence of leaders for acquiescence.

You're a respected educator, Dr. Larken, and you've got to make your position clear. You must provide leadership before the extremists succeed in purging our libraries of anything that provokes thought or dissent. I'm sure you don't want to be remembered as the person who stood by while great literature was expelled from our schools.

We must stand firm against the continual assault and erosion of our basic liberties. Once we're told what we can read, our freedom is gone. Stand up for what you believe in or step aside.

Sincerely,

Seth Powell

- Public opinion can give a politician backbone. Speak up.

- Plant the thought of history assessing the reader negatively. That's a strong incentive to do the right thing.

Name
Address
City, State Zip

Date

Councilwoman Theresa Luganos
Town Hall
588 North Stockard Street
Mt. Laurel, NJ 08054

Dear Councilwoman Luganos:

I have no quarrel with the development of a condominium complex in our area. In fact, I believe a well-built, well-run condo attracts good neighbors and has a positive impact on tax ratables.

I do, however, have one major concern: traffic flow. I've lived in condos in different parts of the country, and I've seen surrounding neighborhoods become literally choked with traffic. There's never enough thought given to access roads. Thousands of cars move through narrow residential streets that were never intended for high volume traffic.

We can avoid endangering children if we simply take a hard look at traffic patterns <u>before</u> construction is started. Will you please work with us to make sure our neighborhoods aren't harmed? If you do, we'll work with you to make the complex a reality.

Sincerely,

Sherman Percival

- A reasoned approach will earn you an audience; ranting and raving will not.

- Concern for children's safety is always taken seriously.

Name
Address
City, State Zip

Date

People for Ethical Treatment of Animals
P.O. Box 42516
Washington, D.C. 20015

Dear P.E.T.A.:

As someone who cares deeply about the humane treatment of animals, I urge you to investigate unethical practices at Jefferson University Research Center in Seattle, Washington.

A reliable source tells me that unanesthetized orangutans are being maimed in head trauma experiments.

The research supervisor is Dr. Emmet Widener. Over the past three years he has received $1.6 million dollars in Federal grants for these experiments.

I'm outraged that my tax dollars are being used to torture animals. Please use your resources to stop the experiments.

Sincerely,

Donna Crocker

- State your position on the research.

- Give as many details as possible about the research. (e.g., location, type of research, project director, etc.).

Name
Address
City, State Zip

Date

Ms. Cynthia Case
News Director, WHY-TV
Barker Square
Philadelphia, PA 19106

Dear Ms. Case:

I was appalled at the graphic footage that appeared on your noon newscast on Thursday, November 3. A public official was shown throwing himself from a window.

Thursday was a snow day and my children were home from school watching television. What they saw on the news upset them so much that they couldn't fall asleep that night.

What was gained by showing that incident to your audience? Have you no sense of responsibility to the viewing public?

I watch the news for information—not to be shocked. You've turned your newscast into a tabloid show.

I won't watch your news broadcasts again. I'm also sending a copy of this letter to your station's General Manager, as well as to the FCC.

Very truly yours,

Marjorie Kolze

cc: Charles Eppley, General Manager, WHY-TV

- State the time, date and specific material that offended you.

- Send a copy of your complaint to whomever you think might influence future broadcasts.

Letter of Support to President (7-09)

Name
Address
City, State Zip

Date

The President
The White House
1600 Pennsylvania Avenue, NW
Washington, D.C. 20500

Dear Mr. President:

I think the media has been unfair to you. Every report I see—in print or on television—seems to paint you with a broad brush, and a negative one, at that.

Of course, nobody likes to hear bad news. But it's far better for you to tell us the truth, negative though it may be, than to invent positive news, just to placate the American people.

I'm someone who <u>approves</u> of what you're doing, and I know there are millions of others who do, as well. Don't let media "gurus" dissuade you from your "Changing Horizons" agenda. It takes courage to initiate change, but the alternative is even more frightening for our country.

To quote Franklin Delano Roosevelt:

"The country needs, and unless I mistake its temper, the country demands bold, persistent experimentation. It is common sense to take a method and try it. If it fails, admit it frankly and try another. But above all, try something."

Keep trying, Mr. President. And good luck.

Sincerely,

Deirdre Saruk

- Tell the President why you think he's doing a good job.

- A quote can often put your own thoughts into more eloquent language.

Name
Address
City, State Zip

Date

The Honorable Rita Hauser
House Office Building
Washington, D.C. 20515

Dear Representative Hauser:

Your recent appearance on "Inside the Beltway" was impressive. You overwhelmed your opponent, and you did it with insight and grace. I applaud you.

Most politicians consult a pollster before taking a stand. You appear to speak from conviction, not out of concern for your ratings in the polls. That's why I want to volunteer for your next campaign.

People like you can make a difference. And you've convinced me that I can make a difference, too.

Thanks for being my Representative.

Sincerely,

Suzanne Bircy-Talone

- Tell the Congressperson what inspired you to write the letter.

- If the reader spurred you to action, say so.

Fan letter to TV Newsperson (7-11)

Name
Address
City, State Zip

Date

Ms. Mariah Morgan
WHAT-TV
Media Square
St. Louis, MO 63116

Dear Ms. Morgan:

You have singlehandedly debunked the myth that female anchors are airheads! You're an intelligent, articulate and incisive journalist.

Over the past few years, I've admired many of your investigative pieces. The most recent one, "Cutting Edge," was a stunning expose, expertly researched and written.

You deserve an award—no—two awards: One for excellence in broadcasting and one for advancing the credibility of female anchors everywhere. Congratulations on a job well done!

Sincerely,

Shari Werther

- Tell the broadcaster what you admire about their performance.

- Refer to a specific accomplishment, if possible.

Letter of Praise to Company President (7-12)

Name
Address
City, State Zip

Date

Ms. Alberta Mikloscik
President
DeLeon Cosmetics Co.
3000 Tropical Trail
Naples, FL 33941

Dear Ms. Mikloscik:

Bravo! I applaud your decision to establish a free, on-site day care center for DeLeon employees. You're doing your part to provide working mothers (and fathers) quality care for their children, while freeing them to concentrate on their jobs.

I'm a working mother with a child in private day care. I spend my days with one eye on the clock—wondering how my son is. His day care center is thirty minutes from my workplace and transporting him back and forth is time-consuming. Needless to say, I can't "drop in" to check on him during work hours. And the added expense of private care takes a huge chunk out of my paycheck.

I hope you will serve as a role model for other local companies. All working moms and dads deserve company-sponsored day care. Just because we have to work outside of the home, it doesn't mean we don't care about our families.

By the way, I'm sending my resume to your Human Resources Department. I'd like to work for DeLeon Cosmetics!

Sincerely,

Bridget Stanza

• Relate why you feel the actions are commendable.

• Tell the company president what prompted you to write.

Fan Letter to Author (7-13)

Name
Address
City, State Zip

Date

Ms.Isabella Estes
c/o Vaneck Publishing Company, Inc.
163 West Avenue
Rochester, NY 14616

Dear Ms. Estes:

Your murder mystery, "The Wellspring," kept me up all night. I'm an avid reader of crime stories and can usually predict the ending. But this plot was so intricately woven that I was stunned at the outcome. What a debut for a first-time novelist!

I particularly liked the character of the mother. It's to your credit as a writer that she was diabolical yet sympathetic!

I expect to see "The Wellspring" on the New York Times bestseller list. I'm doing my part by touting it to all my friends.

I await your next "whodunit."

Kindest regards,

Saundra Aikens

- Tell the author what you admire about their work.

- Express an interest in the author's other books.

Fan Letter to Rock Star (7-14)

Name
Address
City, State Zip

Date

Mr. Billy Rival
c/o Decibel Records
1432 Avenue of the Stars
Los Angeles, CA 90036

Dear Billy:

You're a poet as well as a musician. Your latest hit, "Pack it In," combines a great sound with an important message.

I own all your CD's and have enjoyed watching you mature as an artist. You made a quantum leap from "No Go" to "Speaking My Piece," and now you've scaled new musical heights.

I'm hoping your upcoming concert tour will include a stop in Detroit. You're an electrifying live performer and I look forward to hearing the new songs in person.

Could you send me an autographed picture?

Sincerely,

Cassie Cochran

- Show your familiarity with the artist's music—past and present.

- There's no guarantee that a photo request will be honored, but it doesn't hurt to ask.

Letter of Praise to Athletic Coach (7-15)

Name
Address
City, State Zip

Date

Mr. John Chisholm
Athletic Office
Bradford University
19 University Place
Philadelphia, PA 19122

Dear Coach Chisholm:

I'd like to congratulate you on another winning season as coach of the Bradford Bears. Your patience and determination have guided a young team toward maturity. But I admire you for more than your ability to coach basketball.

Under your guardianship, many disadvantaged young men have been transformed into disciplined, productive individuals. You build character on and off the court.

That's why I love to attend games at Bradford. I'm not just watching a team beat the odds to win a game. I'm watching them beat the odds to win at life.

Thanks.

Sincerely,

Ken Fairchild

- Tell the reader what you admire about them.

- If your admiration extends to characteristics beyond the call of the job, be sure to mention that.

Gift Card One-Liners 8

How many times have you stood at the florist's stand, or at the department store counter, with your mind as blank as the gift card in front of you? Minutes tick by. The clerk impatiently taps a pencil. Finally you sigh in frustration and scratch out those boring old cliches: "Good luck" and "Best Wishes."

A clever gift card message is a condensed version of a well-written letter. It presents its own set of challenges. The first, and most obvious one, is time. Coming up with the perfect one-liner in the few minutes it takes to pay for a gift or send flowers is quite different from sitting at your desk and thoughtfully composing a letter. Secondly, the one-liner has to be succinct. The essence of your message must be conveyed in one sentence.

Here is an opportunity to flex your creative writing muscles. As long as your message is appropriate to the occasion, there's no limit to the ways you can recast the standard "Happy Anniversary," "Congratulations," or "Get Well."

If the circumstances warrant congratulations or celebration, humor and originality can be just as effective as sentimentality. Or the occasion may remind you of a line from a well-known song, or a familiar quote.

Date

Dear Eve,

I knew that you could. I knew that you would. And you did!!!

Congratulations!

Love,

Sherri

• Try a different approach to a standard phrase.

Date

Dear Marva and Will,

You're truly blessed. You've found what many only dream of.

Love,

Shannon and Earl

• Convey your sense of sharing in the couple's joy.

Date

Dear Eleanor and Gene,

You've spoken the vows; you're Mr. and Mrs.
Now you'll discover what marital bliss is.

Warmest wishes on your marriage!

Sincerely,

Val and Edwin Huggler

• Create a message that's upbeat and supportive.

Date

Dear Liza and Malcolm,

If it ain't broke—don't fix it!

Happy Anniversary!

Love,

Ariel and Roger

• Reflect the positive aspect of a lasting marriage.

Date

Dear Lorna and Stefan,

Good things really do come in small packages!
Enjoy your beautiful little bundle.

Sincerely,

Lynn and Gil

• Show that you share in the wonder of the new arrival.

Date

Dear Gretchen,

Stand back, world! Here she comes! Congratulations, Graduate.

Warm regards,

Deanna and Colin Blake

• Make it sound as if the reader is the first person ever to graduate!

Date

Dear Ina and Hal,

May your hearts and hearth glow in the warmth of your new home.

Congratulations and good luck.

Fondly,

Wendy and Theo

• A new home symbolizes a new beginning. Convey the wish that it be a joyful one.

Date

Dear Andy,

Congratulations. Now you can take your "show" on the road!

Happy 16th birthday—and drive safely!

Love,

Aunt Elise

• Acknowledge the significance of the 16th birthday. (For many teenagers it means eligibility for a driver's license.)

Date

Dear Wally,

Once you're over the hill, it's easy sledding. Happy 50th Birthday!

Love,

Doreen

• Show that there are benefits to getting older.

Date

Dear Howard,

Get well quick—it's no fun when you're sick.

Best wishes,

Carlotta

• Make the message upbeat and humorous.

Date

Dear Monique,

Now that your surgery's over, you're perfect!

Love,

Leslie

• Convey a sense of warmth, humor and optimism.

Date

Dear Kathy,

You've achieved success the old-fashioned way:
You've earned it.

Congratulations and good luck.

Best regards,

Florence

• It's okay to use a familiar saying if it expresses how you feel.

Date

Dear Eloise,

May your days be filled with all the joys which had to wait until you had the time.

Affectionately,

Iris Lake

• Acknowledge that retirement presents the opportunity for personal pleasure.

Date

Dear Ronnie,

No special occasion. Just to show my everlasting love for you.

Always,

Stan

• Simplicity often expresses a sentiment best.

Date

Dear Adele and Perry,

Joy at this most beautiful time of the year.

Merry Christmas!

Fondly,

The Friesels

• Express the warmth you feel at holiday time.

Introductions and References 9

Think about the occasions when you've met people for the first time. Do you remember being a little unsure of yourself? Or wishing you had said something you only thought of saying later? One of the great advantages an introductory letter has over a face-to-face first meeting is that it provides the opportunity to craft your first impression. So take your time and be sure you get it just right.

Put yourself in the reader's shoes when you write an introductory letter. The person you're writing to has never met you, but is being asked to like you, understand who you are, agree with you, hire you, or endorse you. The reader can't see your body language or the expression on your face, or hear the sound of your voice. You have to create a picture with your written words. The overall tone of your letter will determine how you are perceived.

Introductions. Consider the circumstances, then decide what tone would be most appropriate. If, for example, you're introducing yourself to the friend of a friend, the tone might be informal or even humorous. If you're a teacher writing to a parent, you'll want to sound cordial and friendly, but somewhat more formal.

If you're writing about something that may be upsetting to the reader, or if your letter of introduction contains a surprise or a shock ("I'm your biological daughter"), try to balance the effect by sounding as calm and reassuring as possible.

References. The person who writes a letter of reference is putting their good name on the line. If you're requesting a letter of reference, realize that you're asking for a significant favor. Explain why you need the reference and how important it is to you.

Even though some might deem it presumptuous, it's reasonable for you to give the writer some "direction" as to the form the reference should take. It's nonproductive to ask for a favor that can't be used because the reader missed the point of the request.

If you're the one who's writing a reference for someone, stick to what you know about the individual. Don't comment on their scholarship, character or work ethic if you've never been in a position to judge them.

We Have a Mutual Friend (9-01)

Name
Address
City, State Zip

Date

Dear Carla,

Our mutual friend, Helene Peters, suggested that I contact you.

I've recently relocated here from Chicago, where Helene and I belonged to the same fitness club. Finding the right place to work out is almost as important to me as finding the right apartment, and I could use your expert guidance.

Helene tells me that you work out almost every day. I'd like to get together with you to hear your recommendations. Perhaps I could meet you to check out your club one evening. I hope you'll telephone me at work: (813) 555-9889 or at home: (813) 555-2136.

I look forward to meeting you, and perhaps to finding a new fitness friend.

Cordially,

Caitlin O'Connor

- Mention your mutual friend by name, and reveal something about the nature of the relationship.

- Establish that you have a common interest with the reader (e.g. fitness, music, theater, etc.).

I'm the Child You Gave Up for Adoption (9-02)

Name
Address
City, State Zip

Date

Dear Mrs. Schaum,

I hope you will be at least a little bit pleased to read this letter, which is very difficult for me to write.

After conducting several months of research I have documented proof that you are my biological mother.

I was born on November 20, 19XX at General Hospital in Baltimore, Maryland. I was adopted by Mona and John Whitman. They have been wonderful parents, but I have always longed to know the woman who gave birth to me.

I am contacting you in the hope that we can arrange a meeting. I don't intend to disrupt your life—I only want to clarify mine.

Will you please respond by letter or telephone (404-555-4763)?

Hopefully,

Beth Whitman

- Don't set the reader up by saying you expect them to be very upset about the news.

- Give reassurance that you don't want to cause distress—you only seek information.

Name
Address
City, State Zip

Date

Dear Regina,

Please forgive me if this letter comes as a shock to you. I don't know how much your parents have told you about your origins.

I am your biological mother. You were born on January 25, 1972 at Bay Bridge Hospital in San Francisco. I was a sixteen year old unwed mother, and at the time I believed I had no choice but to surrender you for adoption. The loss has haunted me all these years, and I felt compelled to find you.

I don't want to interfere in your life—I only seek reassurance that you are all right.

Will you contact me by phone at (714) 555-3218 or by letter?

I await your reply.

With great anticipation,

Mattie Allen-Rogers

- Prepare the reader for the startling news.

- Supply details that confirm the relationship (e.g. date of birth, place of birth, etc.)

Name
Address
City, State Zip

Date

Dear Mrs. Gorman,

You have a bright ten year old! I say that with assurance because I'm Chad's teacher. I enjoy having Chad in my class. He is an imaginative child with exceptional reading ability.

I'm writing to tell you that I welcome comments and suggestions from the parents of my students. Please don't hesitate to contact me if there's something you'd like to discuss.

Sincerely,

Virginia Feeley

- Make a specific reference to the special needs or abilities of the child.

- Establish a foundation for good parent-teacher communication.

Request to Teacher for College Reference Letter (9-05)

Name
Address
City, State Zip

Date

Sonia Lankenau, Ph.D.
All-Girls Choir
1428 South 23rd Street
Boston, MA 02181

Dear Dr. Lankenau:

The All-Girls Choir was an important part of my teen years. It wasn't just the singing that I enjoyed—I also loved the rehearsals, the travel, the concerts, and the friendships that I developed.

I owe you a debt of gratitude for teaching me so much about music and discipline. You've been a motivating force in my life. In fact, I plan to major in voice at college next year. That's why I'm asking for one more favor.

I'm applying to Westminster College, and I need a letter of reference from a music teacher. I feel confident that a recommendation from you would earn me serious consideration by the admissions committee. Just leave the audition to me!

I want to thank you for so many things, Dr. Lankenau. Mostly for showing me that music can be much more than a pastime.

Gratefully,

Rebecca Waterman

• Explain why you're requesting a letter of reference from this reader (e.g., "you've been a strong motivating force," etc.)

• Share your hopes and plans for the future.

Name
Address
City, State Zip

Date

Mrs. Sylvia Freund
Brite Pharmacy
416 Manning Avenue
Kingsville, TX 76543

Dear Mrs. Freund:

Before we moved, I enjoyed working at your pharmacy after school and on weekends. You taught me so much about how a business operates and how to deal with people. Now that graduation is approaching, I'll be looking for full-time work.

Would you provide a letter of reference? I believe it would impress future employers to know that you trusted me to open and close the store and to handle cash transactions. Anything else positive you could mention about my work habits and enthusiasm would also be appreciated.

I'll call you next week to be sure that you're willing to write the reference. If you are, perhaps you can tell me when you'll be able to complete it, because it would be a great help during interviews.

Thanks for everything.

Sincerely,

Gary Davis

- If you're asking for a reference from a past employer, remind them of how pleased they were with your performance.

- By gently suggesting a time deadline, you might help speed up the process.

Name
Address
City, State Zip

Date

Ms. Margo Golden
Golden Touch Marketing
10 Peninsula Boulevard
Seattle, WA 98101   Re: Lydia Wilson-McCune

Dear Ms. Golden:

I understand that Lydia Wilson-McCune has applied for a position as a copywriter with your ad agency. I hope you'll give particular attention to her application. She has much to offer you.

Lydia was my assistant for about a year at Elkman Advertising, where I'm a creative director. During that period, she proved to be an excellent writer, and I encouraged her to pursue a career in that field. She has a flair for the offbeat and the focus to carry a project from concept through storyboard.

I think Lydia has a terrific future as a copywriter. Her husband's relocation has forced her to leave our agency. I hope you'll be able to reap the benefits of her talent.

Sincerely,

Shelly DePaulo

• Give some background regarding your relationship with the person being referenced.

• State your evaluation of the person's qualifications for the new job.

Name
Address
City, State Zip

Date

Dear Neil,

I inquired about membership in the Cherry Valley Country Club, and the executive director, Monte Parker, was very encouraging. However, he said that before membership could be considered, I must first submit a letter of introduction from a club member.

May I ask you to write a letter on my behalf? It should comment on the length and type of our relationship (e.g., we're business and social friends), a statement of my character, and any comments you would like to make about my family and financial status. I'm not sure you should mention how poorly I play golf! That might get me blacklisted.

If there's any problem whatsoever about doing this, please let me know. Otherwise, I'll thank you in advance. This is a great favor, and I'm very appreciative of your help.

Cordially,

Gary Kiner

- When asking for a letter of introduction or a reference of any kind, it's a good idea to suggest what you'd like the writer to say.

- Make it hard for the reader to say no. Tell them, in advance, how grateful you'd be for the favor.

Invitations 10

Although invitations may vary as much as the occasions for which they're used, there are some features that they all must contain. If the questions below are all addressed, your invitations—formal or informal—will always be understood and acted upon:

WHO? Name of celebrant and host (if someone other than the celebrant is giving the party).

WHAT and WHY? Type of event, for example retirement dinner, anniversary brunch, or child's birthday party.

WHEN? Date and time.

WHERE? Place.

RESPONSE REQUIRED? R.S.V.P. or phone call.

Invitations to formal occasions should have traditional wording and style, but most other invitations—adult's or children's—are limited only by imagination.

Adult invitations. When you send an invitation, you're really trying to persuade someone to come to the event, so make your appeal as strong as possible. Entice the reader visually to motivate them to attend. Using stationary or card stock in attractive colors and type faces evokes a positive reaction.

Most people love parties and special occasions, but sometimes it takes a real sales pitch to bring the attendees to an event. That's especially true if there's a charge involved, as with a fundraiser or community party, for example. With these, pull out all the stops when preparing your invitation to make the reader feel they'll be missing out on something very special if they don't attend. Give the reader some details about what will make this year's class or family reunion different—and better—than others, or how they'll be able to talk directly with the candidate at a political fundraiser. That's the way to get fence-sitters to make the decision to join you at your gathering.

Make it easy for the invitee to respond to your invitation. If you enclose a response card in a self-addressed, stamped envelope with a check-off or easy to fill in reply card, your response rate will increase dramatically. A deadline for responding will also help. For smaller events, you may choose to request a telephone response.

Children's invitations. Young children are delighted to receive mail. Always send party invitations directly to the child, even if it's a three year-old. Most parents will make it a point to give the envelopes to their children so they can see their names and react to the invitation.

For a children's party, be sure to explain the event as completely as you can—including starting and ending times, special clothing or equipment to be brought, and what food or activities may be expected. Children's invitations should contain bright, creative, playful and unusual visual and verbal messages to make them appealing.

Jack Morton and Melissa Morton-Crowley
invite you to join them
as they honor their father
Harold Morton
on the occasion of his
60th birthday.

Reception and dinner
Saturday, the seventh of May
at 7:00 O'clock
in the Sterling Hotel
East Ballroom
7 Oak Avenue
Santa Clara, CA

R.S.V.P. (408) 555-9508 by April 18

- Be sure to mention if there will be food service.

- There should be a deadline for responding.

Rehearsal Dinner for
Carolyn Garner and Michael Went
Hosted by
Mr. and Mrs. Bernard Went
Friday, June 13, 6:30 p.m.
The Hideaway Restaurant
South Hannibal, NY 13074

R.S.V.P.   The Wents
W. Litton Street
Cleveland, OH 44179
(216) 555-8508

- A rehearsal dinner is usually given by the groom's parents the night before the wedding.

- Traditional invitees are the wedding party (and, often, spouses). In many cases, out-of-towners (particularly, close relatives) may be invited.

Allison Winters Bernbach
and
Joseph Alexander Alesio
request the pleasure of your company
at the celebration of their marriage
Saturday, the eleventh of February
nineteen hundred and ninety-five
at six o'clock
Regency Park Hotel
San Francisco, California

R.S.V.P.   *Black tie requested*

- The phrase, "honor of your presence" can be substituted for "pleasure of your company."

- A self-addressed stamped response card usually accompanies the formal invitation.

Mr. and Mrs. Charles Alexander
request the honor of your presence
at the marriage of their daughter
Julia Marie
to
Mr. Ward Francis Landy
Saturday, the fourth of September
Nineteen hundred and ninety-six
at half after eleven in the morning
Our Lady of Assumption Church
20 High Avenue
Charleston, South Carolina

R.S.V.P.

- This is the standard formal wedding invitation; however some of the language may be changed. For example, the bride and groom may want to issue the invitation themselves.

- An invitation to the reception is usually presented on a separate piece of stationery.

Name
Address
City, State Zip

Date

Dear Uncle Mort,

Harvey and I would be so pleased if you could join us as we celebrate our marriage in the presence of a small gathering of friends and relatives.

The ceremony will be in the garden of my parents' home on Sunday, May 22, at 2:00 P.M. Harvey's uncle, Judge Wyndham, will officiate. A small reception at the house will follow immediately afterward.

We look forward to sharing our wedding day with you. Please let us know by May 12 whether or not you can come. You may telephone me at (405) 555-1140. If no one is home, please leave a message on the machine.

Love,

Helena

- Stating that only a select group of close family and friends is invited makes the reader feel their presence really matters.

- Since the wedding itself is rather informal, the R.S.V.P. can be informal, too.

Name
Address
City, State Zip

Date

Dear Amy,

You're one of the very few people I'd like to have witness my marriage to Darryl. You've been to my first three weddings, and I'd like you to see me do it right for once!

We'll be married on Sunday, April 22, in the Emerald Suite of the Providence-Carstairs Hotel, at 1:45 p.m. (directions are enclosed). Refreshments will be served.

The only gift I want is your presence (bring a guest, if you'd like). Call me at (401) 555-2603 to let me know if you can make it. Please try; it would mean a lot to me.

Love,

Caroline

- By the time you've reached a fourth wedding, standard rules need not apply. Invitations can be as informal as a letter, or as formal as an engraved invitation.

- Advise if no gifts are to be given.

Name
Address
City, State Zip

Date

Dear Barbara,

Ssshh! It's a surprise!

Shana is celebrating her fortieth birthday on March 6, and I'm having a dinner party for her that night. I'm inviting some of her closest friends. Can you join us?

I'm asking everyone to meet at my house no later than 7:00 p.m. Please park in the mall lot across the street so Shana won't suspect anything. She'll be arriving with Diane at 7:30. (She thinks the three of us are going out to dinner.)

Please let me know if you can attend by calling me at home (201) 555-6589 or at work (201) 555-3500 no later than February 28.

We're pooling our resources to buy her that microwave she keeps talking about, so if you're agreeable, please send me a check for $25 for your share.

And remember—it's a surprise!

Best,

Marni

- Emphasize the need for secrecy.

- State what is requested of the invitee (for example, parking a car out of sight or chipping in for a gift).

Name
Address
City, State Zip

Date

Dear Aunt Jewel and Uncle Leo,

We're celebrating our twenty-fifth wedding anniversary with a renewal of our vows on Saturday, September 5. We hope you'll be with us at 11:00 a.m. at the Cathedral of Sts. Peter and Paul, 21st Street and Kinney Boulevard. Immediately following, we'd like you to join us for a luncheon at the Springhouse Inn, directly across the street.

Please let us know by August 16th if you will be able to attend. Call us at (718) 555-4002 or write to the above address. Your presence would add special meaning to the occasion.

With love,

Brenda and Jim

- Informal invitations may be handwritten and individualized for each recipient (usually reserved for small functions).

- It encourages attendance when you tell people that their presence is important to you.

Mr. and Mrs. Cary Norton
are obliged to recall their invitations
to the marriage of their daughter
Lynne Grace
to
Mr. August Sparks
as the marriage will not take place

- Though printed or engraved announcements may be sent, if time does not allow, do whatever is necessary to get the notice out—including sending handwritten notes, telephoning, or sending overnight letters.

- If illness is the cause of the recall, you may wish to say so to avoid undue speculation (e.g., due to the illness of their daughter...).

IT'S A BABY SHOWER

For: Linda Hauser
Date: March 15
Time: 2:00 p.m.
Place: The Riley Residence
142 Stenton Lane
Arvada, CO 80002
Given by: Linda's sisters,
Megan Riley and
Marcy Parrish

Let's shower Linda with baby gifts that befit a princess—
she's having a girl!

Call Megan at (303) 555-7355 to R.S.V.P. by April 30

- Include the baby's sex if it is known (and if the parents give permission); it helps in the gift selection process.

- There are many potential additions to a modern invitation. For example, to acknowledge the parent's wishes, you may request gifts of only cloth diapers or cotton clothing.

A white christening gown our baby will wear
On this wonderful day when he's placed in God's care.

Christening Celebration for
Charles Edward Foster, Jr.

Date: Sunday, November 14, 1995
Time: 4:00 p.m. (refreshments and buffet)
Place: The Foster Residence
14 Melbourne Street
Reston, VA 22091

R.S.V.P. (301) 555-5798

• This is an informal invitation, which is perfectly appropriate for home-based celebrations. However, if you're planning a larger, more formal function, a more formal invitation—similar to one used for a wedding—should be considered.

Mr. and Mrs. Amos Jordan
cordially invite you
to share their joy
as their daughter
Mary Catherine
makes her first communion.

St. Helen's Cathedral
Ivy Lane, Stockbridge, Michigan.
Mass will be held on Saturday,
May 3, at 10:00 a.m.

Luncheon immediately following
at the Jordan residence
6 Lancelot Court,
Stockbridge, Michigan

R.S.V.P. (517) 555-5622 by September 9

- To simplify matters for out-of-towners, be sure to include directions to each locale.

- If you're planning to send printed invitations, you need to allow at least 4-6 weeks lead time prior to the mail date.

Invitation to Family Reunion (10-13)

(Page 1...)

"If a boy is a lad and he has a stepfather, is the boy a step ladder?"

Best Groaner, 19XX Reunion
Winner: Uncle Frank Weston

Were you there when Aunt Dorothy fractured her foot when she kiddingly (?) kicked Uncle Sam?

Happened during the 19XX Reunion
(Does Dorothy still have a limp?)

Did you see cousin Wendy get hit in the eye with a watermelon seed during the family seed spitting contest?

A 19XX event. (Wendy married the
emergency room intern who treated her.)

(Page 2)

IT'S FAMILY REUNION TIME AGAIN!

Do you want to risk missing out on this year's fun? Who knows what might happen next? Here's the vital information:

McLeester Family Reunion
Sunday, July 13, from 11:00 a.m.-6:00 p.m.

Olympia Lakes Amusement Center
(BBQ grills available)
Route 280
Bridgewater, NJ 08807

(Conveniently located just 1/2 mile from the Kennedy Hospital Emergency Room)

R.S.V.P. Carl McLeester (609) 555-3312 by June 20

- A corny invitation like this will remind family members of the unique quality of your family—and should encourage them to attend your upcoming reunion.

- An informal invitation can be printed on two pages, or on one folded page—like a greeting card with writing on the first and third sides.

Come to
An Old Fashioned Neighborhood Barbeque
Hot dogs, Hamburgers, Horseshoes and Beer
Bring your Appetite and your Loudest Bermuda Shorts
Games and Prizes

Four o'clock Saturday, August 5
The Bradley's
826 Piedmont Way

Call if you can't come
555-3198

- This invitation gives a lot of specifics in a lighthearted, friendly way. The reader knows who will be at the party, what will be served, what the activities will be, and what to wear.

- Clearly state what kind of response, if any, is expected.

Name
Address
City, State Zip

Date

Dear Dale and Danny,

Stan and I have decided that the only way to escape the winter doldrums is to give in to them: build a fire, mull some cider and cook up a big pot of stew. Then invite some friends over to share it all.

Will you join us for a cozy surrender to January?

Please come on Saturday, January 12 at 7:30 p.m. I'll call you this week to confirm.

Hope you can make it!

Fondly,

Irene

- In the absence of an "official" special occasion you can create one by the tone of the invitation.

- For any invitation that doesn't have an R.S.V.P., be sure to arrange for some kind of confirmation if it matters to you whether or not a guest will be accepting.

Name
Address
City, State Zip

Date

Dear Valerie and Sean,

Frank and I are planning to be at our country house the weekend of October 20th and 21st, and we'd love to have you join us. The fall foliage is gorgeous around that time, and the drive should be spectacular. We have no special plans, but if you enjoy the outdoors, there's a great hiking trail just down the road.

Come in time for lunch on Saturday, and stay through an early supper on Sunday. Lumberville is about a two-hour drive from the city, so if you leave around 10 a.m.you should arrive just in time for our famous fajitas!

We're very casual (even when we go into town for dinner), so bring comfortable clothes: jeans, slacks and sweaters are fine. A jacket is a good idea, too, because the autumn nights can get chilly!

We hope you can make it. Give us a ring by Friday of this week at (215) 555-3381 to let us know. We'll give you directions then.

Warmly,

Reba and Frank

- When inviting guests for a weekend, spell out the terms of the invitation, including arrival time, departure time and which meals are to be served.

- Give a general idea of what activities to expect, and what wardrobe is appropriate.

Name
Address
City, State Zip

Date

Dear Janice and Mel,

John is being given a special "Award of Merit and Excellence" at his company's annual meeting, and he's invited his close friends and relatives to share in his accomplishment.

The enclosed invitation from his company gives all the details, except one: how much it would mean to both of us if you could come. You've been great friends to us, and we'd love to have you with us on this special occasion.

I hope you can make it. In addition to the presentation, it promises to be a wonderful night of dining and dancing. Send in your response, as indicated, but also, please give me a call to let me know if you're coming.

Love,

Ruth

- Invitations to most awards functions are sent by the organizations but you can personalize them by adding handwritten or typed notes to special friends and relatives.

- Be sure to tell the invitee to honor the formal response request. Otherwise their place may not be held at the function.

Herb needs time to read a good book,
To smell the roses, take a lingering look.
He wants to travel the U.S.of A.
To hike a trail, swim Montego Bay.
Now that he's leaving his office environment,
Join us to celebrate Herb's impending retirement.

Retirement Dinner Party for Herb Wingate
Given by his children (Gail Lister and John Wingate)

Date: Friday, August 17
Time: 6:30 p.m.
Place: The Mansion, 422 W. Smalley Pike
        Littleton, CO 80120

R.S.V.P. by August 1 (303) 555-7981 (The Lister house)

- You can set a festive mood, even before the party starts, by sending an upbeat invitation.

- Include the names of the party-givers, so guests know who is hosting the party.

Name
Address
City, State Zip

Date

Dear Jamie,

Zeke Guyer will be in town the week of April 15 to promote his new novel. He's going to steal a few hours from his hectic schedule to join us for a small dinner in his honor. I'm inviting a group of friends from his pre-bestseller days, and you're at the top of the list.

We're meeting at Tiramisu, on Abraham Street, at 7:30 p.m. on April 18. Please let me know if you can attend (and if you'll be bringing a date) by calling me at (405) 555-7595 no later than April 11.

I look forward to reminiscing with you, and I know that Zeke does too.

Warm regards,

Mariette Fonda

- State the reason for the get together, and tell why the reader's presence is important.

- Indicate whether or not it's appropriate to bring a date.

Name
Address
City, State Zip

Date

Mr. Alphonso Barillo
4717 Marble Rock Road
Davenport, IA 52802

Dear Mr. Barillo,

I'm delighted to invite you to join a select group of community leaders to spend an evening with the woman who we believe will be the next Governor of Iowa, Barbara Clark Chasen.

Representative Chasen has asked me to organize a small pre-caucus dinner party at my home on Sunday, September 18 at 6:00 p.m.

This will be a unique opportunity for you to speak directly to the candidate. Representative Chasen will spend time at each table, sharing ideas with you and other supporters—all of whom represent the heart of the Davenport community.

Please circle the 18th on your calendar to reserve the evening for cocktails, dinner and conversation with Barbara Clark Chasen. Your contribution of $1,000.00 per person will go a long way towards ensuring Representative Chasen's election as the next Governor of Iowa.

Please respond by returning the enclosed card by September 1. See you there!

Warm regards,

Darlene Sawyer Sims
Iowa Campaign Chairwoman

- Stress the importance of the fundraising event.

- Assure the reader that there will be a benefit to them in attending.

Name
Address
City, State Zip

Date

Dear Classmate,

What do a lawyer, exotic dancer, plumber, college professor, travel agent, circus performer, accountant and funeral director all have in common? They're your classmates from Northwestern High School's 19XX graduating class...and they'll all be part of a nostalgic evening of reminiscing, dining, dancing and guessing who's who.

Here's Part I of NW's Great Reunion Evening: Match the classmate with the occupation. Send your answers along with the enclosed acceptance card and you may be the winner of a $500 savings bond (announced at the reunion)!

19XX Yearbook Job Prediction	Current Occupation
A. Selma Blank (research pharmacist)	1. Lawyer
B. Thomas Parnell (dancer)	2. Plumber
C. Hazel Butler (tennis pro)	3. Accountant
D. Don Gottschalk (engineer)	4. Exotic Dancer
E. Lisa Grauten (photographer)	5. Funeral Director
F. Richard Kuttner (politician)	6. Circus Acrobat
G. Robert Maynard (pilot)	7. Professor
H. Steven Tanner (teacher)	8. Travel Agent

There will be lots of fun on Saturday, February 23, starting with a reception at 5:30 p.m., followed by dinner and dancing at 6:30, at the Oakland Street Catering Hall (details on the enclosed information sheet). Reserve your place now. Find out who's doing what...and more!

Enthusiastically,

Larry Severola, Class of 'XX

- Think of a reunion invitation as a sales letter, because its asking people to spend money. Give reasons to attend.

- Curiosity is a great motivator for attending a reunion.

*Shelly loves crafts and bright, jazzy clothes
So a T-Shirt design bash is the party she chose!*

Come to Shelly O'Connor's 10th Birthday Celebration!

*Saturday, August 4, 2:00-5:00 p.m.
Where: Crafty Ann's Emporium
8 Country Crossing
Morgantown, PA 19543
(party room is in the rear)*

*You'll receive your own pastel T-Shirt, as well as paint,
glitter, decals and sample designs, to make your own
fashion statement. Birthday cake and other party refreshments
will be served!*

*Say YES to an afternoon of fun and fashion
at Shelly O'Connor's 10th Birthday Party.*

R.S.V.P. (215) 555-0503 by July 27

- There are many unique facilities, offering interesting activities, that now cater to kids' parties. A quick look through the Yellow Pages will help you throw a memorable party. (Try Party Planning Services or, if your child has a particular interest, look under that category.)

- Be creative with the invitation. Perhaps the facility can give you pictures and suggest wording to include.

WANTED: Josh Kolchins

FOR: A birthday Bar-B-Q for Phillip Lombardi

LAST SEEN: In Miz Horne's second grade posse

Kolchins is instructed to give himself up at 2:00 p.m. on Saturday, June 10. Sheriff's deputies will be waiting at the Lombardi Ranch, 24 Winding Way, Townshend, Vermont.

REWARD: Ice cream, cake, games, and a chance to win a real cowboy hat!

Ring us up at the Lombardi Ranch by June 3 to say if you'll show: 555-8865

- Don't just state the theme of the party. Elaborate on it throughout the invitation.

- Some form of R.S.V.P. is required, even for children's parties.

All goblins and all ghoulies
All monsters, spooks and crones,
On brooms or feet, come trick or treat,
We'll dine on skeleton's bones!

The date's all Hallow's evening
The Haunted House is mine;
To get a shock, come at six o'clock
And plan to shriek 'til nine!

R. S. V. P. by October 25

Bobby Ruttenberg
(212) 555-6547

- With an amusing invitation like this, the fun starts even before the party begins.

- Give the date, time and address without breaking the theme mood.

Name
Address
City, State Zip

Date

Dear Samantha,

I'm having a slumber party on November 20 and I hope you can come.

Bring your sleeping bag, your warmest P.J.'s and your cutest stuffed animal. We're taking over the recreation room for the night.

I know it's called a slumber party, but don't plan on sleeping!

Come at 7:00 p.m. We're sending out for pizza at 8:00. See you then (I hope!). Let me know by November 13 if you can come (555-4024).

Love,

Kelly Slawek

- Tell the reader what to bring to the party.

- If the party begins around mealtime, state whether the invitation includes food.

Name
Address
City, State Zip

Date

Dear Jason,

I'm having a pool party, and you're invited!

Bring your bathing suit, a towel and a brown bag lunch. (We'll have drinks and dessert.)

Date: July 8, 19XX
Time: Noon
Address: 1 Apple Orchard Terrace

R.S.V.P: (503) 555-6620 by July 5

The party is on even if it rains. We'll be all wet anyway!

Please come!

Your friend,

Jamie Schertzer

- Be specific about what the reader should bring to the party (e.g. towel, picnic lunch, etc.)

- Indicate whether or not there is a rain date.

Invitation for Child to Spend Weekend (10-27)

Name
Address
City, State Zip

Date

Dear Jessica,

Can you spend the weekend of May 23 at my house?

We're planning to open our pool then and I want you to be here for the first swim of the season. There's a hitch, though.

Before we can swim, we have to help my mom and dad remove the pool cover. It's a big job but it's fun, too. And the reward is that we get to swim all weekend.

We can pick you up on Friday night after dinner and bring you home Sunday afternoon. Call me at 555-6831 to let me know if you can come.

Love,

Kelsey

- Describe the activities planned for the weekend.

- Make arrangements for transportation.

Letters to Builders and Landlords 11

Contractors are generally honest, hardworking people who sometimes make errors because they have so many details to manage. It's best if you can establish an amiable, rather than an adversarial relationship with them from the start. If you don't ask for the impossible, if you stick with the agreed upon deadlines, materials and fees, and make some allowances for the occasional error, you should be able to maintain a fine relationship with the folks who are doing construction work for you. The same is true for most landlords—a good relationship will work to your benefit.

Builders and contractors. A home represents the largest expenditure most people will ever make. So if things go awry when you're undertaking construction or remodeling of your house, the impact can be enormous, both financially and emotionally.

Begin to protect yourself from unforeseen occurrences by getting all information and agreements in writing. If you're promised something verbally, follow up with a letter stating what was said, and asking for confirmation. Then if something does go wrong, you have a good chance of correcting the situation by using the written agreement to guide, encourage, motivate, or threaten action, if necessary.

Deadlines, materials, numbers of workers and responsibility for repairing manufacturing defects should be part of any understanding. Often, while a job is in progress, you or the contractor might think of an enhancement or two. Don't just give a verbal "go-ahead," no matter how good you feel about the work. You need to agree in writing about the specifics of the changes, including costs. Builders and contractors who are unwilling to give you what you want in writing—including references—are not worth the risk.

Landlords. Occasions arise where you need to ask for something you'd like or something that's owed to you by your landlord. Don't always make the assumption that the landlord will be unwilling to do what you want. In some cases, you can gain compliance or favors by being creative. Try to think of ammunition that will convince a landlord to work with you. Can you offer a promise to extend or renew your lease, in return for a favor? It can be of value to mention a positive as a counterpoint to a negative. And remember, the problem that's plaguing you may not be your landlord's fault. Blame a power or phone outage on your local utility and save your displeasure with your landlord for things over which they have control.

If you know you're dealing with an irresponsible or obstinate landlord, using an assertive tone may help stir action. List the history of your past attempts at solving a problem (phone calls, meetings), including time frames and unmet deadlines. The more you have on paper, the better the chances you'll succeed if you need to seek legal redress later on.

Name
Address
City, State Zip

Date

Mr. Wilbur Grant
Master Remodeling, Inc.
1328 Willits Avenue
Grand Rapids, MI 49441

Dear Mr. Grant:

You're receiving this letter instead of a signed agreement because the 25-year guarantee we discussed was not included in your contract. As soon as you produce the completed document, written specifically to fit this job, I'll sign and return it to you with the initial check.

I'm looking forward to getting started.

Sincerely,

Sonny Weber

• Don't get into a narrative of who said what when. Just state your concern.

• By promising a check, you're likely to get action. If that doesn't work, find another contractor.

Name
Address
City, State Zip

Date

Mr. Owen Cwalina
Murray's Nursery and Landscaping
1110 W. Brinton Road
Caribou, ME 04736

Dear Mr. Cwalina:

I appreciate the time and thought that went into the plans for our grounds, but I'm not sure we can afford to do everything at once. So I'd like you to resubmit your quote, breaking the pricing down as follows:

o Regrading/installation of French drain
o Addition of a sprinkler system (front and back)
o Landscaping and Spring clean-up around new porch
o Landscaping and trimming at rear property fence

We'd like to make a quick decision. To save a day or two, please fax your revised quotation to my office (207) 555-3887. Be sure to mark it to my attention.

Thanks for your patience. I'll be in touch.

Sincerely,

Barry Reisling

- Be specific as to what you want broken out, or you may frustrate yourself and the contractor.

- Often, a contractor will drop the overall price, rather than lose an element of a job.

Name
Address
City, State Zip

Date

Mr. Clayton Thomason
ATCO Builders
4136 Wayland Avenue
Norman, OK 73069

Dear Clayton:

I like everything about your proposed contract except the payment schedule. I'm reluctant to give you what amounts to 90% of the total by the time the job would be only 50% completed.

Here's what I suggest:

Upon agreement	20%	($6,000)
In two weeks	20%	($6,000)
In four weeks	20%	($6,000)
Upon completion	40%	($12,000)

If you agree, send a revised contract and I'll return it with two signatures: one on the agreement, the other on a check for $6,000.

Thanks for working with me.

Sincerely,

Walt Petrocelli

• Virtually any aspect of an agreement is negotiable. Don't be afraid to ask for better terms.

• The prospect of immediate cash is a strong incentive to make changes quickly.

Name
Address
City, State Zip

Date

Mr. Lloyd Yarnall
Century Contractors, Inc.
10 Garrison Plaza
Billings, MT 59105

Dear Mr. Yarnall:

Thank you for giving my husband and me the opportunity to consider your proposal for the addition to our house.

Your ideas are impressive, but we've decided to hire a builder who has more experience refurbishing older homes.

However, we've recommended you for another job. An acquaintance of ours is soliciting bids for a master bedroom suite. We've given him your business card.

Good luck and thanks for your time.

Very truly yours,

Mrs. Yvonne Palmer

• There's no need to detail the specifics of your decision.

• The offer of a referral is a friendly gesture.

Name
Address
City, State Zip

Date

Mr. Gabriel Koch
ABC Roofing Company
855 W. Paoli Avenue
Sparks, NV 89431

Dear Mr. Koch:

You might not think that a couple of missing shingles are of cosmic importance. But my porch roof looks lousy without them and I expect a leak any day.

I've now been waiting six weeks for you to send someone to finish what appears to be a 15-minute job. (I didn't have to wait five minutes for you to appear whenever a payment was due.) I'm frustrated, not just because you haven't completed what you contracted for, but because you haven't had the courtesy to respond to any of my calls.

I don't understand why you would jeopardize your reputation over something so small. If my roof isn't finished by the May 12th, I'll contact the Better Business Bureau and town construction officials.

Sincerely,

Lance Spiegel

• Recount the reason for your disappointment or frustration.

• Make it clear that your patience has a time limit.

Name
Address
City, State Zip

Date

Mr. Rosco Arnolfini
Arnolfini Paving
214 High Street
Muncie, IN 47305

Dear Mr. Arnolfini:

Every spring I see news reports about fly-by-night contractors who do lousy work—then take the money and run. It's made me a cautious consumer.

I hired you to pave my driveway because your price seemed fair and you had good references. Now I'm questioning my judgement. Only two weeks have elapsed since you completed the work, yet my driveway is cracking.

I want you to come back and do the job right.

I've left five messages on your answering machine, but you haven't returned my calls. If I don't hear from you by the end of the week I intend to report you to the Better Business Bureau, the Consumer Advisory Board and the Department of Consumer Affairs.

You can contact me at work: (317) 555-8000, or at home: (317) 555-0907.

Very truly yours,

Madeleine Harris

- Tell the contractor why you're dissatisfied with the job and how you want it to be corrected.

- State what you intend to do if your demand isn't met.

May I Keep a Pet in My Apartment? (11-07)

Name
Address
City, State Zip

Date

Ms. Felicity DeMoss
181 N. Wellington Street
Fort Wayne, IN 46809

Dear Ms. DeMoss:

Would you agree that Tim and I have been model tenants? The rent is always paid on time, we don't throw wild parties, we help with the upkeep of your lawn, and we're active in neighborhood affairs.

I've recited that partial list to justify asking for a favor. My sister is moving to Canada and can't take her cat with her. I'd like your permission to bring the cat here.

Melissa is a house cat. She's never been out of my sister's home, and would never leave my apartment. She's de-clawed, so she couldn't do any harm to the apartment. As you know, Tim travels quite a bit and I'd like to have a pet to keep me company when he's gone.

I'd be happy to sign a waiver against any damage. This is very important to me, and I really need you to say "yes."

Very truly yours,

Lois Barney

• There's nothing wrong with asking for a favor in return for "good behavior."

• Explain the circumstances and the import you attach to the request.

May I Sublet My Apartment? (11-08)

> Name
> Address
> City, State Zip
>
> Date
>
> Mr. Douglas Maloney
> Cottonwood Springs Apartments
> 4300 W. Oakmont Street
> Edgewood, MD 21040
>
> Dear Mr. Maloney:
>
> My company has offered me a one-year assignment in Saudi Arabia. This is an important opportunity for me, and I want to say "yes." But I can't afford to pay for housing there and here. So, before I say yes, I need your permission to sublet my apartment.
>
> As you can tell from a check of my record, I'm a responsible tenant. And I'll bring you someone who will maintain an equally prompt payment schedule and good neighbor policy. Since I'll be resuming my lease when I return, I obviously want to do everything possible to be sure you're pleased with whomever replaces me.
>
> I must let my company know by next week if I can take the Middle East job. That means I need to hear from you no later than Monday or Tuesday. I'll call for your response. Please be positive; you'll have no regrets.
>
> Cordially,
>
>
> Bertram Witherspoon

- The best technique is to be pleasant, and hope the landlord will comply.

- Give a firm deadline for an answer.

Would You Let Me Out of My Lease Early (11-09)

Name
Address
City, State Zip

Date

Mr. Delmar Herrmann
Pheasant Run Apartments, Inc.
522 Harbour Drive
Sherwood, MD 21030

Dear Mr. Herrmann:

When Nina and I leased our apartment, we hadn't planned on having children. Two-and-a-half years later, we have two!

I know we have six months remaining on our lease but, as you can imagine, we've run out of living space. And that's an understatement. We don't have a legal leg to stand on, but we're appealing to you to let us out of our lease.

While our preference would be to find a home, we'd be willing to move to a larger apartment within Pheasant Run if that would satisfy our obligation. But it's imperative that we find more spacious quarters quickly...while we still have a shred of sanity.

We're in your hands, Mr. Herrmann.

Hopefully,

Stewart Brooks

- Don't make threats when you have no negotiating position.

- Most people are willing to help others in need. It's up to you to ask in a way that evokes compassion and, hopefully, cooperation.

Name
Address
City, State Zip

Date

Mr. Harry Braman
Cedar Crest Corporation
218 W. Delanco Street
Philadelphia, PA 19123

Dear Mr. Braman:

As I look out my bedroom window at a snow-covered parking lot, it seems as if the world is at a standstill. Nothing is moving.

The problem is, that as I and hundreds of other tenants sit trapped in our apartments, we're able to watch television and see that the rest of the city is back in action. Major arteries are open, side streets are navigable, and walking doesn't seem any more perilous than usual.

Even after repeated phone calls to your office, you have not lived up to your end of the lease agreement by plowing the lot and access roads to the highway. Many of us have missed work along with much-needed income.

This isn't the first time you've been slow to respond to our needs, Mr. Braman. But I promise you that you'll be suffering along with us if this pattern of neglect continues. Perhaps a rent strike will better convey our frustration than words.

Sincerely,

Sarah Manning

• It's always helpful to point out that dissatisfaction is based on a contractual—rather than an emotional or ethical—violation.

• Threats can be effective if the recipient believes you have the power to deliver on them.

My Apartment is Overdue for a Paint Job (11-11)

Name
Address
City, State Zip

Date

Manager
Clairmont Estates
Route 58 at Jackson Avenue
Ft. Wayne, IN 46952

Dear Sir or Madam:

According to my lease, my apartment is to be repainted every three years. But I've been here for 41 months, and I haven't been advised that your painters are planning to do the work.

Perhaps I should have contacted you earlier, instead of waiting to be notified. In any case, please accept this letter as confirmation that I want my apartment painted, as promised in our agreement. I'd appreciate it if the job could be scheduled and completed within the next 30 days.

May I hear from you next week? Please call me at my office during the day (219) 555-2000, ext. 223, or in the evening at my apartment (219) 555-0448.

Sincerely,

Carla Quenton

- Explain the issue in the first paragraph.

- There's no need to be accusatory. Just tell what you want and when you want it.

Name
Address
City, State Zip

Date

Mr. Ned Armstrong
Fox Hollow Apartments
728 Cedar Hollow Road
Rapid City, SD 55705

Dear Mr. Armstrong:

Because you've been so uncooperative, my attorney has directed me to place all future rent payments in an escrow account. When the water pressure problems and leaks are finally resolved, he'll be happy to discuss disbursement.

If you have any questions, please contact my attorney directly:

John O'Hara, Esq.
Butterfield and O'Hara
4200 Skyway Drive
Rapid City, SD 55702
(605) 555-1900

Let's get this resolved right away, shall we?

Sincerely,

Damon Cornwallis

- Once you've engaged an attorney's help, let them handle negotiations and interactions. Simply refer the landlord to the attorney.

- Rent escrow accounts are an acceptable method for making unreasonable people act reasonably.

I'm Frustrated By Your Unresponsiveness (11-13)

Name
Address
City, State Zip

Date

Mr. Colin Althorp
Manager
Silver Manor Apartments
4611 White Horse Road
Waterloo, IA 50706

Dear Mr. Althorp:

I'm not sure which is more frustrating: my broken refrigerator or your unwillingness to deal with it.

Since I started calling you three days ago, I've had to throw out all my food, and I've done without ice. And I still have no idea when you plan to fix it and reimburse me for my losses.

Since you have an aversion to answering my calls, I'll have to take matters into my own hands. If I don't hear from you by the end of this week, I'll bring in my own repairman and subtract the cost from future rent payments. And there had better not be a complaint about the cost.

Very truly yours,

Anton Burnett

- Let the reader know what action will be taken, and when it will happen.

- Send the letter via an express service so the reader receives it in time to take action. This also gives you proof of delivery.

Name
Address
City, State Zip

Date

Mr. Sanford Kimball
Prescott Hall Apartments
1 Presidential Boulevard
Groton, MA 01471

Dear Mr. Kimball:

I need your understanding and patience for about 30 days.

One of my freelance accounts just sent me a note (attached) advising that they're changing accounting procedures. This change-over will cause them to be approximately 30 days late with their payment.

I was expecting a substantial check from that company this month. Without it, I can't pay my rent. So will you work with me? Will you accept 50% payment this month, and let me make it up next month? This is a short-term cash crunch which will resolve itself by the end of next month.

I'll be grateful if you'd make allowances during this temporary setback.

Very truly yours,

Vicki Wendlestadt

• It's better to inform your landlord of an impending problem and to ask for help in resolving it, than to wait until it escalates into a crisis.

• Assure the landlord that the difficulty is temporary,

```
                           Name
                          Address
                       City, State Zip

Date

Mr. Edward Dreyer
Bridgeton Management Corp.
4610 Walnut Lane
Gretna, LA 70053

Dear Mr. Dreyer:

Your refusal to return my security deposit is pushing me to take
legal action. I'm sure neither of us wants to incur attorneys' fees,
but I don't know what else I can do to force you to return the $450
you owe me.

After four years of an excellent tenant/landlord relationship, I can't
understand what has prompted this poor-faith action on your part.
I followed the lease to the letter: No pets, no permanent alter-
ations, no wallpaper. I even spackled the few nail holes I made.
There was no damage of any kind; you had nothing to do to
prepare the apartment for the next renter.

You won't receive any more calls or letters from me. I'll wait until
November 1, and if I haven't received a check for the full $450, I'll
let my attorney work it out for me. If you want to call, you can
reach me during the day at (504) 555-0959.

Sincerely,



Oliver Markham
```

- Although appeals to reason rarely work with unreasonable people, it's worth reminding the landlord of your impeccable tenant record.

- Let the landlord know that you are willing to pursue the matter, even if it means incurring legal costs.

Letters to Professionals 12

Dealing with professionals can be intimidating for a number of reasons. Doctors, lawyers, accountants and other service professionals often speak in technical terms that may be indecipherable to laymen. In addition, some professionals have an air of self-importance or even arrogance. And finally, the circumstances under which most people have to deal with professionals are often stressful—an ailment, a law suit, a tax audit.

Professionals depend on your patronage, just as other business people do. Yet, many people are uncomfortable questioning a professional. Individuals who have no problem returning damaged goods or withholding payment for shoddy work, often lose their nerve when confronting professionals. A well written letter will hold a service professional as accountable as any other "supplier" with whom you do business.

Doctors. You might expect that physicians would be constantly vigilant, to ensure that their practices run smoothly and that their patients are pleased with the service they receive. Yet, many people say that their doctors are unaware of problems with their staff, their billing procedures or their own demeanor.

Surprisingly few people make these complaints directly to their physicians, and things are unlikely to change unless the physician is given a reason to change them. Letters that suggest potential loss of patients, reputation and billings are strong motivators.

Lawyers. Some lawyers use the skills they learned in law school to put you at a disadvantage. They can turn phrases cleverly and couch their answers to your questions in obscure or evasive terms. Don't be put off by these techniques.

Ask as many questions as you need to, until you satisfy any doubts you might have about your representation (e.g., How many of these types of cases have you undertaken? How many went to trial? What were the results? What do you consider to be your specialty?) And demand that the answers be in plain language that you can understand. If you're dissatisfied with the service you've received, let the lawyer know that you have "reasonable doubts" about them and that you plan to take your business elsewhere.

Accountants. Accounting can sometimes be as much an art as a science, and if you feel your accountant has missed the boat in guiding you, or has led you astray, you need to question them. You needn't start out by being antagonistic; just raise the issues you wish to have addressed. It's important that you have confidence in your financial advisor.

If you've ever had a dispute over fees, you understand the importance of having costs quoted in writing. Even hourly fees can be misleading if there's no estimate of the number of hours required to perform the work. If you can't get a written quote from an accountant or other professional, you might want to start looking elsewhere.

Name
Address
City, State Zip

Date

Hedda Moore, M.D.
122 South Danforth Street
Detroit, MI 48233

Dear Dr. Moore:

Our conversation has left me confused and anxious. You told me that my condition was "serious." You also told me that I have "nothing to worry about." Which is it?

I need written clarification from you on the following:

1) What is the exact nature of my condition?
2) What is the best treatment for my condition?
3) What is my prognosis?

Please answer my questions candidly and in language that I can understand.

Thank you.

Sincerely,

Ann Copperman

- List the questions that you would like answered.

- Request that the answers be forthright and in layman's terms.

Name
Address
City, State Zip

Date

Herbert Walker, M.D.
Santa Fe Medical Center
Desert Drive
Santa Fe, NM 87501

Dear Dr. Walker:

Could you please explain the charges on my bill dated August 19.

I visited your office on that date for a throat culture, but I've been charged $165.00. I know we're in the midst a of health-care crisis, but this is ridiculous!

I'm going to withhold payment until I receive clarification. Please review your records and have someone from your office call me with an explanation. I can be reached at the following numbers:

Work: (555) 666-5000
Home: (555) 351-7997

Thank you.

Very truly yours,

Juanita Esparza

- State the reason for your inquiry.

- Say that you're withholding payment pending an explanation.

Send My Records to Another Doctor (12-03)

Name
Address
City, State Zip

Date

Walter M. Adamczyk, M.D.
Orthopedic Associates, Inc.
Rt. 73 and Brick Road
Kansas City, KS 66115

Dear Dr. Adamczyk:

I appreciate the time and thoroughness you've put into my examination, testing and recommendation for surgery. However, before I agree to any invasive procedure, I'd feel a lot more comfortable if I obtained a second opinion.

To help me reach that comfort level, please have a copy of my complete records sent to:

Dr. Richard Grossman
Hardaway Medical Center
48 N. Brighton Avenue/Suite 2A
Kansas City, KS 66111

After I meet with Dr. Grossman, and he confers with you, I'll call you to discuss the next step. Thanks for your help.

Sincerely,

Johanna Corliss

- Many people feel it is a slap in the primary physician's face to request a second opinion, and they avoid taking that important step. In fact, most physicians will gladly provide the name of another doctor for a second opinion, if it's requested.

- Keep your request cordial and non-confrontational.

Name
Address
City, State Zip

Date

Albert Telgheider, M.D.
Mercy Medical Building
888 Glenbrook Road
Kansas City, MO 64157

Dear Dr. Telgheider:

I've been taken advantage of. I arrived at your office in pain last Thursday, with my back in spasm. I was ushered into an examining room, instructed to undress, and assured that you would be with me "in a few minutes."

I couldn't sit on the stool provided because it had no back support. I couldn't lie on the examining table because lying down was too painful. I couldn't return to the waiting room (at least it had comfortable seating) because I was undressed. I waited for you for fifty minutes. When you finally arrived you were brusque and unapologetic.

The Hippocratic oath includes "never abusing the bodies of man or woman." I feel abused, physically and mentally.

You'll need to convince me that what I experienced last week did not accurately represent the way you run your practice, or I'll never seek your services again. I hope to hear from your office.

Sincerely,

Carl Ehmling

• Be descriptive about your frustration. It strengthens your position.

• Explain the consequences of the behavior that disturbed you.

Your Nurse Wasn't Supportive (12-05)

Name
Address
City, State Zip

Date

Waylon Hecksher, M.D.
2 Bala Plaza
Portland, ME 04101

Dear Dr. Hecksher:

Your nurse, Mrs. Barnett, handled my recent phone call to your office in a callous fashion.

I called on Tuesday to learn the results of my Pap smear. Mrs. Barnett informed me the test was positive, and scheduled me for an appointment to see you. When I expressed concern about my condition, she cut me off, saying that you would discuss my situation when I came to the office.

I spent an hour fighting off panic and contemplating my great misfortune.

I called back for clarification, and a different nurse pulled my records and assured me that the this test often produces false-positive results, and that the need for a retest is not at all uncommon.

I'm still unnerved by Mrs. Barnett's insensitivity. She needs to be instructed that patients are naturally worried when they hear about medical problems, and that everything possible should be done to allay their fears.

Very truly yours,

Margo Keating

• Describe how you were mistreated.

• Relate the emotional impact the treatment had on you (and might have on others).

Name
Address
City, State Zip

Date

Gertrude Lindquist, M.D.
Duluth Medical Center
Suite 24
Duluth, MN 55806

Dear Dr. Lindquist:

What ever happened to the care in health care?

When I telephoned you last Friday for reassurance about my upcoming surgery, you were brusque to the point of rudeness. As a result, I felt foolish for expressing apprehension about my operation.

This isn't the first time your phone manner has offended me. I need to feel that my physical and emotional well-being are important to you. If that's asking too much, perhaps I should start looking for another doctor.

Very truly yours,

Heidi Wilson

• Be candid about how the offensive behavior affected you.

• Let the reader know that they risk losing you as a patient.

Your Insensitivity Offended Me (12-07)

Name
Address
City, State Zip

Date

Harold Borler, M.D.
Paoli Memorial Medical Building
Paoli, PA 19301

Dear Dr. Borler:

When my father passed away in January, I telephoned your office to inform you and your staff of his death. Your receptionist assured me that she would give you the message.

My dad was your patient for many years, and I was surprised that you never contacted me to express your condolences.

I was particularly offended, however, when your receptionist telephoned a few weeks ago to schedule a physical exam for my father. As you can imagine, the conversation left me unnerved.

I don't know whether to blame the oversight on poor interoffice communication or insensitivity, but I believe you owe me an apology.

Sincerely,

Amy Rodack

• Tell the reader why their behavior offended you.

• Request an apology.

Name
Address
City, State Zip

Date

Dr. Sandra Waggoner
Abington Medical Group
578 S. Route 52
Abington, PA 19001

Dear Dr. Waggoner:

While I feel you have excellent medical skills, you and your staff are so short on people skills that I've decided to change physicians.

My move is based on three factors:

1. There's no respect for my time. Every visit involves at least a one-hour wait. There has to be a way to better anticipate your time with each patient.

2. Your receptionist acts perturbed whenever anyone approaches her with a question.

3. Your medical technician is rude, and has a heavy hand. She's drawn blood from me three times and has bruised my arm severely each time. An expression of pain is met with a roll of her eyes.

I suspect you wouldn't put up with this sort of treatment from <u>your</u> personal physician (or any other professional). Unless you take some positive steps—soon—mine won't be the only such letter you receive.

Sincerely,

George Agajanian

• A physician is selling a service. If you're not happy with the service, express dissatisfaction, just as you would with any other service provider.

• By listing your complaints, you increase the chances that your letter will be read completely.

Name
Address
City, State Zip

Date

Meredith O'Hara, M.D.
2770 Ranchero Plaza
Amarillo, TX 79109

Dear Dr. O'Hara:

You've restored my faith in the medical profession. I wish that your style of doctoring was universal.

Your sensitivity and concern during my recent illness made a lasting impression on me. I'm sure it helped to speed my recovery.

"Bedside manner" seems to be a lost art among many doctors today. But you have it. And I'm very grateful.

Thankfully,

Hazel Freeport

• Express your appreciation for the special care.

• Tell how you were affected by the concern that was shown.

Name
Address
City, State Zip

Date

Schuyler C. Glenby, Esq.
Feingold, Soble, Reid and Prouser
8888 Warren Circle
Birmingham, AL 35203

Dear Mr. Glenby:

Your attitude at our preliminary meeting yesterday only advanced the stereotype of the greedy, arrogant attorney.

Before asking even one question about the nature of my case, you stated your retainer requirements. Then you launched into a ten-minute tribute to your litigation skills. When you finally turned your attention to me, and I began (somewhat painfully) to relate my story, you interrupted me twice to take phone calls.

When I hire a service professional, I need to feel that he or she will be on my team. Since you made no attempt to reassure me that you had any interest in my case other than financial, I'll be seeking counsel elsewhere.

Very truly yours,

Cecile Cipriani

• Make your point at the beginning of the letter.

• Let the reader see their actions from the standpoint of the client and tell what action you plan to take.

Name
Address
City, State Zip

Date

Arthur I. Herschel, Esq.
Herschel, Fein and Hartshorn
157 Lexington Avenue
New York, NY 10016

Dear Mr. Herschel:

You've lost a client.

I understood that the purpose of a retainer fee was to retain your services—that is, to purchase your attention <u>and</u> your availability.

Last week I needed to speak to you on an urgent matter concerning my company's lease. I placed several calls to your office throughout the day. Although I emphasized the critical nature of the calls, each time your secretary said you were "unreachable."

You did not return my call until <u>three</u> days later. By then, it was too late. The deadline for resolving the issue in my favor had passed.

Please return the $15,000 dollar retainer fee I recently paid you, along with all files, records and paperwork pertaining to my case by next Friday, April 23.

If I don't receive the check and documents I have requested, you and I will still have our "day in court"—but we'll be opposing one another.

Very truly yours,

Shelby Moffet

• Tell the reader why they have lost you as a client.

• If you seek restitution, tell what kind, and state your intention to follow up.

Name
Address
City, State Zip

Date

Mr. Alfred Delaney
Delaney and Smathers
8207 Washburn Avenue/Suite 202C
Allentown, PA 18195

Dear Mr. Delaney:

I'm disappointed in both of us. I should have asked you how much experience you had in criminal law, and you should have told me without being asked.

It was quite a shock to find that I'm being defended on a case of criminal trespass by someone who specializes in divorce cases. You should have told me in advance that you had no experience in that area of law, and referred me to someone with a record of achievement in criminal practice.

Please accept this letter as notice of your dismissal. And don't waste your time sending an invoice. If you do, I'll make a formal complaint to the Pennsylvania Bar Association Ethics Committee.

Sincerely,

Arliss George

- Detail your complaint, particularly if there may be further action taken by you or the attorney.

- A "cause and effect" statement is very powerful (e.g., "If you send an invoice, I'll go to the ethics board.")

Name
Address
City, State Zip

Date

Ms. Elaine Whitman
Whitman and Rowe
58 Arnold Terrace
Eden Prairie, MN 55344

Dear Ms. Whitman:

In the seven months you've been handling my case, I've seen you once. At that initial meeting you impressed me with your credentials and your competence. You never mentioned that all work on my behalf would be performed by a paralegal.

Since then, I have made five calls to your firm and had three follow-up meetings. In each case, I asked for you and was intercepted by your paralegal. The last time I looked, my monthly legal bills had your name as the payee, but I can't imagine why. Your paralegal fields all my questions, has apparently done all the research, and has filed motions and paperwork on my behalf.

It's obvious that my case isn't important to you. Unless you can convince me by the end of this week that I should continue to use you—not your paralegal—I will seek new counsel. I'm very disappointed in your lack of interest and follow-up.

Sincerely,

Helen Montana

- Unless you speak up, nothing will change. If you're not being treated as you wish, it's up to you to take steps to correct the situation.

- The threat of loss of income is a powerful motivator.

Name
Address
City, State Zip

Date

Mr. Dennis Tessla
Tessla and Assoc., P.A.
446 South Broad Street
Kingsford Heights, IN 46346

Dear Dennis:

As you know, I'm very involved with Kingsford Hospital, and serve
as its fundraising chairperson. This unpaid position requires a
tremendous amount of driving time, as I go to meetings with
potential donors throughout the county.

On one of my driving trips, a fellow volunteer mentioned that he
took a $1,200 mileage deduction on his tax return. As we spoke
about it more, he was surprised that I had never taken advantage
of this allowable. I told him my accountant had never mentioned
it.

Is he right, Dennis? Have I been missing a significant deduction
every year? Please check my returns and call me immediately. If
there was an oversight, can we recover for previous years?

Waiting to hear from you,

Samuel Wheeler

- Don't jump to conclusions based on information offered by a nonprofessional. Your
circumstances may be different from theirs.

- A calm, reasoned request will bring about a reasoned response. Your primary objective
is to get an accurate answer.

Name
Address
City, State Zip

Date

Alan Foster, CPA
3900 Palisades Boulevard
Santa Rosa, CA 95401

Dear Alan:

I don't understand your current invoice. It's nearly 30% higher than previous invoices, and there's no explanation attached.

I can only assume this was sent in error because we've never discussed an increase in rates or services. Will you please have your billing department issue a corrected invoice at the usual rate? As always, it will be paid promptly.

Cordially,

Brad Mosbach

• Never accept an invoice for higher than the negotiated rate without asking for an explanation.

• Treat the incorrect invoice as an error. You have nothing to lose, and you might stem an increase by doing so.

Praise and Thank You's 13

In a society where time is measured in nanoseconds, and communication has been reduced to your machine talking to my machine, the value of a personally written note of thanks or praise can't be overestimated. A well-composed thank you letter is more than just an expression of gratitude. It's more than a spur-of-the-moment, easy-to-make phone call. It's written proof that civilized society is not entirely obsolete.

Praise. Whether you're praising a life saving rescue effort or a well-coordinated church bake sale, the purpose of the praise letter is to tell the reader how their actions effected a change for the better. While the objective of this type of letter is to make the reader feel appreciated, don't make the error of being excessively effusive, or you'll be perceived as insincere.

Describe what you admire about the reader's actions—be specific—and relate how those actions affected you on a personal level.

Thank you's from adults. Keeping in mind that the objective of the thank you letter is to make the reader feel appreciated, acknowledge the need or desire that the reader fulfilled. Describe the positive results of the gesture and how it affected you. Finally, if appropriate and possible, offer to reciprocate in some way.

Thank you's from children. A child's thank you letter should look and sound age-appropriate. A perceptive reader will quickly detect the "voice" of a letter from a child that has been dictated by an adult. Talk your child through the thoughts that they want to express in their thank you. Then act as a gentle guide to help the youngster write the letter in their own words.

Thank you's in business. When writing a business thank you, the degree of familiarity or formality with which you address the reader should be dictated by the closeness of your professional relationship. Refer specifically to the event or circumstance for which you're appreciative.

Thank you's to organizations. A cordial approach should be used when writing a thank you letter to an organization. Bearing in mind that the letter may wind up on the company bulletin board, make your thank you all-inclusive, so that each employee will feel appreciated. Convey your belief that the organization's good deed will have far-reaching effects.

Name
Address
City, State Zip

Date

Dear Mark,

As graduation nears, I want to tell you why I always knew that you would be successful. Not just in academics and sports, but in your personal relationships.

One day, when you were 8 or 9, there must have been 20 boys in our back yard playing baseball with you. As I watched from inside the house, I saw little Joe Benjamin (who was thought of as the neighborhood nerd) timidly approach you and ask if he could play.

Most of the other boys started hooting at Joe, calling him names and telling him to go home and play with dolls. As Joe choked back tears and turned to leave, you stood up to the whole crowd. I remember it as if it were yesterday. You announced that Joe was your friend, and that anyone who didn't want to play could leave.

I knew then that you would always have the courage to do the right thing...and I've never been disappointed. You've accomplished virtually every goal you've set for yourself throughout school, and I'm confident that you'll achieve equal success in the work world.

You deserve everything good that's come to you. I'm very proud of you. You've made fatherhood a joy for me.

Love,

Dad

• A description of a significant act or event is an excellent way to illustrate why someone is praiseworthy. (It gives meaning to the words, "I'm proud of you.")

• People never tire of hearing compliments, even if you think they must already know how you feel about them.

You Showed Patriotism (13-02)

Name
Address
City, State Zip

Date

Dear Joey,

When I saw you salute the flag after you received your medal, I cried.

I'm proud of you for "serving with distinction," especially since public opinion wasn't always on your side during the recent conflict. Your loyalty is heartening—even inspiring. I wish more young people felt the same passion you do.

Congratulations, Sergeant Calvo. And thank you for awakening a patriotism in me that's been dormant for too long.

I salute you.

Admiringly,

Paulina Schroeder-Hunt

• Acknowledge the achievement or endeavor that prompted the letter.

• Give the reader a sense that their actions command respect.

You Showed Courage (13-03)

Name
Address
City, State Zip

Date

Dear Jerry,

When your mother told me how you and your friend pulled someone from a burning car, I felt weak in the knees. What a remarkable, selfless act.

While there's a part of me that wants to tell you never to put yourself in that kind of danger again, it's overruled by the part that admires your courage.

Uncle Marv and I are very proud of you. You deserve all the praise that's been coming your way.

Love,

Aunt Fay

• Recognition from family members is cherished.

• Demonstrate that you know just what the accomplishment was.

Name
Address
City, State Zip

Date

Dear Heather,

Your "new and improved" school transcript is testimony to the power of commitment. Congratulations!

You took responsibility for your academic situation and set out to improve it. You succeeded. What a giant step toward maturity.

I'm so proud of you. I look forward to celebrating your future triumphs. There are sure to be many of them.

Love,

Mom

• Acknowledge the commitment that was required to bring up the grades.

• Convey your feeling of confidence in the reader.

You Led the Team to Victory (13-05)

Name
Address
City, State Zip

Date

Dear Thad,

I'm still hoarse from cheering! Your winning touchdown was the most exciting moment I've seen in high school football. You must have jumped five feet to make the interception.

It was a thrill to see you in action. Your ability to perform under pressure is impressive and demonstrates not only your serious athletic ability, but also your nerves of steel. You're a hero to your classmates and your friends.

Congratulations on a great game!

Sincerely,

George Serota

- Compliment the reader on their specific skills.

- Acknowledge the effort required to win the game.

Name
Address
City, State Zip

Date

Dear Matthew,

Your quick response when Uncle Frank began having chest pains probably saved his life.

I'm so grateful that you insisted on calling the ambulance despite Uncle Frank's protests that he was only experiencing "indigestion." Your composure and resolve (while the rest of us were barely functioning) were remarkable. You could teach a course in crisis management.

Thank you for taking charge. I don't want to think about what might have happened if you hadn't been there.

Love,

Aunt Molly

- Let the reader know that their response affected the outcome of the crisis.

- Make a specific reference to the action that made a difference.

Name
Address
City, State Zip

Date

Dear Mrs. Barry,

Robbie struts to the school bus these days, and his new confidence is thanks to you.

Prior to your tutoring sessions, Robbie was restless and unmotivated. Computer games had triumphed over good study habits, and Rob's grades reflected that. Now he's transformed, and the credit is yours.

Your work with Robbie has been a successful blend of teaching, psychology and cheerleading. Thank you for helping him to understand the subject matter, and even more importantly, thank you for helping him to feel good about himself.

Sincerely,

Karen Jones

• Give some background that puts the reader's contribution into perspective.

• Describe the positive changes that have resulted from the reader's efforts.

Name
Address
City, State Zip

Date

Dear Gavin,

Thanks to the care you provided for Dad, his morale has received a boost and so has mine. We both needed some "R and R!"

Taking care of him is a full-time job. I often feel that I'm the parent and he's the child. The responsibility eventually wears me down, and that's why I appreciate your giving me a "breather."

It's great to know that I can count on you.

Sincerely,

Maggie

- Express the positive results of the care.

- Praise the reader for being someone you can depend upon. This leaves the door open for future requests for assistance.

Name
Address
City, State Zip

Date

Dear Trish,

It's taken me almost a week to even begin to realize how much you've done for me and my family since Tom was injured.

You've handled everything, from seeing to it that the kids were taken care of, the right people notified, our home looked after, mail and deliveries sorted, parents called and calmed, and heaven knows what else.

You've made it possible for me to concentrate on Tom's recovery and deal with doctors, nurses, rehab centers, police, lawyers, insurance agents, and dozens of other people and details. I don't know how I'll ever be able to thank you.

You're a dear friend, and I'm very, very grateful for everything you've done.

With great affection and appreciation,

Peg

- People who come through for you in a crisis should be told how much their contribution is recognized and appreciated.

- Acknowledge just what was done for you.

Name
Address
City, State Zip

Date

Dear Evelyn and Jack,

You two are special people. Although we've received so many wonderful Christmas cards and greetings, your donation to the American Cancer Society in our name really stands out as capturing the essence of the season.

Thank you for the thought. We hope you both have a particularly healthy and prosperous New Year.

Fondly,

Suzanne and Cal Worth

- Always recognize a gift/contribution/donation in writing.

- Refer specifically to the cause.

Name
Address
City, State Zip

Date

Dear Jim,

I felt at home at your party even though you were the only person I knew. I was so comfortable, so relaxed, and had so much fun that it seemed as if I were with old friends. I thoroughly enjoyed getting to know everyone.

The food, by the way, was wonderful, too. You're a remarkable host, and I hope you'll allow me the opportunity to reciprocate soon.

Thanks again for a terrific evening.

Cordially,

Jerome Czerny

- Select something about the party to comment on (e.g., guests, food) in addition to saying "thank you."

- A suggestion of reciprocity is an indication that you enjoyed yourself.

Name
Address
City, State Zip

Date

Dear Gene,

I'm usually skeptical when someone insists I see a favorite movie or read a much-acclaimed book. The reality never seems to match the expectation. But the book you lent me was an exception. It left a mark.

I had heard of Bernard Malamud, but had never read any of his books. If the rest of his works approach the standard set by The Fixer, I have a lot of catching up to do.

Thanks for insisting!

Cordially,

Joe

- People love to have their recommendations (books, movies, restaurants, etc.) endorsed.

- Don't write a book report. Just tell the lender you enjoyed it.

Name
Address
City, State Zip

Date

Mr. Daniel Thomson
34 Alcott Rd.
Mobile, AL 36633

Dear Mr. Thomson,

I never thought that supporting the rights of high school children to read books such as <u>Tom Sawyer,</u> <u>The Last of the Mohicans,</u> and <u>Catcher in the Rye</u> would generate such scorn and loathing.

Just when I was wondering if the self-righteous zealots who packed the school board meeting were going to tar and feather me, you joined my team. And that was all it took. Emboldened by your support, others gathered their courage. Eventually, we were able to force a withdrawal of the censorship motion.

Thank you for your willingness to stand up for a principle. I know this fight isn't over, but now we have the nucleus of a group that should be able to withstand the onslaught of the book-burners.

I'll be in touch.

Very truly yours,

Barny Lockwood

- Explain why the support meant so much to you.

- Describe how the reader affected the outcome of the event.

Thank You for My Wedding (13-14)

Name
Address
City, State Zip

Date

Dear Mom and Dad,

I've attended many weddings that reflected what the parents wanted, but you let Will and me make our wedding our own. You were so supportive and helpful through the whole planning and preparation period that you made the actual event a joy for everyone.

I don't know what the wedding cost—you never let me worry about it—but I know it was a stretch. I'll never forget what you did for Bill and me, and how you helped me begin married life exactly as I'd always hoped.

With all my love and thanks,

Gretchen

- By writing a letter of thanks, you're giving a memento that may be saved and re-read again and again.

- Weddings are often stressful. Comments about supportiveness during this period are much appreciated.

```
                        Name
                        Address
                     City, State Zip

Date

Dear Len,

Thank you for being so sensitive to our needs.  It was really
thoughtful of you to offer financial help, but we're confident that
we can weather the storm.

Sarah's job is solid, and as long as we continue to keep a tight
rein on our expenditures, we'll be fine.  I plan to take part-time
work until something opens up for me again.  Being an eternal
optimist, I know that a good job is just around the corner.

You're a great friend, Len.  We appreciate your caring about us.

Fondly,



Dan
```

- An offer to help monetarily should not be taken lightly. Be sure the reader understands that you feel good about the intent. Don't let pride stand in your way.

- Although you do not have to give a reason for refusing a cash gift or loan, an explanation can be very reassuring to the individual making the offer.

Name
Address
City, State Zip

Date

Dear Joanne,

Thanks for the final payment. From what I've heard, it sounds as if your business is back on its feet. And that makes us so happy.

Just remember: If you ever run into a cash crunch again, we expect you to come back to us for help. We may not be wealthy, but we have enough to help our favorite niece.

Let us know how things are going. Will we see you at the family reunion in San Angelo?

All our love,

Aunt Felicia and Uncle Roy

- When the final payment of a loan is made, thanks are in order (from both parties).

- If the dealings were satisfactory, you might suggest that the family "safety net" will remain in place.

Name
Address
City, State Zip

Date

Dear Judith,

When I awoke after surgery, I thought I was in a garden! There was a beautiful blur of pink and white next to my bed.

Now that I'm fully alert, I can appreciate the arrangement you sent even more. The sight of all those lovely tulips and roses has lifted my spirits.

I'm feeling stronger each day. Thank you so much for the thoughtful gift and encouraging words.

Fondly,

Deena

- Express how much the thoughtfulness meant to you.

- Make a specific reference to the flowers (for example, "tulips and roses" or "basket of daisies."

Name
Address
City, State Zip

Date

Dear Jeff,

You're the best listener! You remembered that I said I never had enough steak knives when company came over. And you also have great taste: The Honnenger set you gave me is perfect. I can't wait to use it during my next dinner party.

Thank you for a very thoughtful gift.

Fondly,

Laurie

• An enthusiastic response by the recipient of a gift pleases the giver and rewards the effort they put into the choice.

• Noting you're aware that the person paid attention to something you said adds a personal touch that's often lacking in thank you notes.

Thank You for Gift, to Relative (13-19)

Name
Address
City, State Zip

Date

Dear Aunt Anne,

It's hard to believe the magnificent crystal candlesticks you gave us have survived bombs over London, a trans-Atlantic journey to the United States, the Depression, and four generations of Babcocks!

Mark and I will keep these cherished treasures in the family, in accordance with your wishes. And we'll display them prominently in our home. They're so beautiful, we want to share them and their history with everyone.

You could not have given us a more wonderful or appreciated gift. Thank you so much.

With love and affection,

Cecilia

- A meaningful "thank you" is often based on relating your understanding of the gift's significance. For example, if a family heirloom is given, show your appreciation of its history by retelling the story.

- Assure the giver that their gift is important to you, and that any directives attached to the gift will be honored.

Thank You for Baby Gift (13-20)

Name
Address
City, State Zip

Date

Dear Mia,

The photo album you sent was beautiful! Where did you find it?
The lovely antique lace cover just invites people to look at it.

I can't wait to start filling the album with pictures of Chelsea.
Thank you for a gift that will contain wonderful memories for us.

With appreciation,

Joy

- Comment on at least one aspect of the gift.

- If possible, tell how it will be used.

Name
Address
City, State Zip

Date

Mr. Craig Edwards
Scarborough Enterprises
1870 Birchmont Road
Billings, MT 59101

Dear Craig:

You've been just what the doctor—or a higher authority—ordered. You've brought a business sense to the church board, and you've helped put us on a firm financial footing for the first time that Reverend Dayman and I can remember.

Because of your vision and skillful management ability, we've been able to expand many programs, the most important of which has been our day care facility. It's had the effect of attracting lots of young families first to the center, and then into the church.

I knew you'd make a contribution as a board member, but I had no idea how substantial it would be. Speaking as a friend, I hope that our growth has been as rewarding to you as it's been to me and the entire church community, and that you'll continue your leadership role for many years to come.

Thanks for everything. You're an inspiration.

Sincerely,

Andrew Hopson

- One reason people do volunteer work is for the thanks they get. If you give it to those who deserve it, they'll continue to work on your behalf.

- Offer a specific example of a praiseworthy accomplishment.

Name
Address
City, State Zip

Date

Dear Charlie,

I just completed my first round of golf as a member. I played as poorly as ever, but somehow it felt better!

Thank you for sponsoring us; being a part of Richland Hills means a lot to me and my family. Ellen and I would like to say thanks by having you and Carolyn over for dinner. I'll call you shortly to see when we can mesh schedules.

I'm pleased that our business friendship has turned into a personal one.

With heartfelt thanks,

Kevin

- When someone does a good turn for you, make it a point to tell them how much it means to you.

- A major favor may warrant a tangible acknowledgement, such as a dinner invitation or a gift.

Name
Address
City, State Zip

Date

Dear Tom,

Henry Wadsworth Longfellow said, "A single conversation across the table with a wise man is better than ten years' study of books." By that measure, I must have the equivalent of five or six Ph.D.'s.

Without your guidance, I'd still be struggling with my life, chasing after all the wrong things. With your help, I've become secure in myself and my faith. And now that I have my personal life in order, material rewards are starting to follow.

You've been more than my minister, Tom. You've been my life support system. Thanks for helping me find my way.

With deep respect,

Hugh French

- Mentors of any stripe usually find their reward in the helping; however, a letter of thanks may be the best affirmation of all (other than seeing your personal growth).

- The thanks becomes more meaningful when you explain how the relationship/mentoring has changed things for you.

Name
Address
City, State Zip

Date

Dear Louis,

Sometimes a problem can be overwhelming. That's when the advice of a trusted friend is invaluable.

I was so baffled by my predicament that I didn't think there was a solution. Your wise counsel proved me wrong—what a relief!

I feel lucky to be the beneficiary of your wisdom and experience.

Thank you.

Gratefully,

Charlene

• Express your gratitude.

• Indicate to the reader that the advice paid off.

Name
Address
City, State Zip

Date

Dear Phil,

It's been a heck of a year for me, hasn't it? I've lost my mother, been divorced from my wife, wrecked my car, switched jobs, and moved. And there are still two months to go!

The only thing I could always count on was that you'd be there for me. Whenever I needed a go-between with Doreen, you were there. When I foolishly tried to drown my sorrows in a glass of beer, you drove me home. If I needed to talk about my job, family, or the meaning of it all, you were willing to listen.

I sometimes felt that I would have needed a padded cell if it hadn't been for you. You're a great friend, and I appreciate everything you've done for me. I owe you a lot, and I won't forget it.

Gratefully,

Gordon

• Even though people help people because they want to, it's rewarding to receive a heart-felt "thank you."

• Mentioning what was special to you is appreciated.

Name
Address
City, State Zip

Date

Dear Gail,

It's easy to be a friend through the good times. The real test of friendship comes during adversity.

Thank you for your unwavering support during the awful period I've just gone through. You listened without judging. You made me laugh. You dragged me to the movies!

You have my respect, my admiration, and my gratitude. When I "grow up" I want to be just like you!

Love,

Mimi

• Tell the reader why you appreciate the friendship.

• Give examples of what the friend has done for you.

Name
Address
City, State Zip

Date

Dear Kevin,

When my other "friends" called in sick on moving day, I wanted to climb into one of the empty crates and stay there.

Then you and your buddies appeared at my door, ready to work. I was so grateful and relieved. Your hard work and enthusiasm rescued me from disaster.

I'd like to repay all of you. How about dinner at my new apartment? I'll call you this week to set a date.

Thank you, Kevin.

Gratefully,

Suzanne

- Express your appreciation openly.

- Suggest a way you'd like to repay the favor.

Name
Address
City, State Zip

Date

Dear Ms. Shearer,

You can't imagine how thrilled I was to receive my acceptance to Northwestern University. And your letter of recommendation was a very important addition to my application.

Attending Northwestern has been my goal since sixth grade. Their drama program is outstanding, and now I'll have the opportunity to participate in it!

I don't know how to thank you enough for writing such a glowing description of me. But I'll remember you each time I take a bow in a Northwestern production.

Gratefully,

Holly Krashes

- Acknowledge the importance of the favor.

- Convey a sense of your gratitude.

Name
Address
City, State Zip

Date

Dear Hal,

Thanks for the most relaxing vacation I've had in years. Your house provided the perfect setting for unwinding. I spent two weeks contemplating sunlight and moonlight on the changing tides. It was blissful.

The house is ideally situated between the ocean and the bay—especially from the vantage point of the hot tub. (But I guess you know that!)

I appreciated every amenity—from the sauna to the automatic ice-maker.

You own a piece of paradise. I'm so thankful you invited me to share it. When you see me, you'll hardly recognize the revitalized version of your "burned-out" friend.

Fondly,

Monique

- Refer to specific aspects that appealed to you.

- Express gratitude for the invitation.

Name
Address
City, State Zip

Date

Dear Arlene and Len,

I know you think we're a little (a lot?) crazy for refusing to kennel our dogs. That makes us even more appreciative that you were willing to babysit for Freckles and Choco last weekend. Without your help we couldn't have attended our nephew's graduation party.

Thanks a million. We owe you one...or two!

Your devoted friends,

Ashley and Mike

• Comment on why the help was appreciated (e.g., special event).

• Make it clear that you're ready and willing to reciprocate.

Name
Address
City, State Zip

Date

Dear Miss Obermyer,

I like having you as my teacher for three reasons:

1) You always answer my questions and never make me feel stupid for asking them.

2) You read stories with a lot of expression.

3) You sent me a card when my dog died.

Thank you for being my favorite teacher. I hope you like having me in your class as much as I like being there.

Love,

Andrea Korman

• Tell the teacher exactly what you like about them. Your thoughts can inspire them to become even better at their job.

Name
Address
City, State Zip

Date

Dear Mr. and Mrs. Shanahan,

I had such a good time at the seashore that I didn't even miss my parents! I loved swimming in the ocean every day and walking on the boardwalk at night. Rehoboth Beach is a neat place.

Thank you for taking me on vacation with you. You made me feel like a part of your family.

Gratefully,

Chloe

• Describe what you liked best about the vacation.

Name
Address
City, State Zip

Date

Dear Mr. Forgione,

The overnight hike was so much fun that now I'd like to sleep outside all summer.

I felt proud that I learned how to pitch a tent and build a campfire. But the thing I enjoyed most was telling ghost stories in the firelight!

Thank you for teaching me how to be a good camper.

Your friend,

Blair Luppold

• Tell what you learned as well as what you enjoyed.

Name
Address
City, State Zip

Date

Dear Mrs. Blackburn,

I thought I would be sad while my parents were away. Instead I was happy. You took such good care of me that the week passed quickly. I had fun too.

You make the best spaghetti I've ever tasted. And I like your parakeet, Sky.

Thank you for letting me stay with you. I hope I'll be invited again.

Love,

Jaclyn

• When you tell the reader exactly what you liked about staying with them, they know you put some extra thought into writing the letter.

Thank You for Gift, from Child (13-35)

Name
Address
City, State Zip

Date

Dear Aunt Georgia,

Do you have ESP? You always give me the present I'm hoping for.

I've already watched the "Snow White" video three times. I'm going to memorize all the songs and sing them to you.

Thank you for being such a good mind reader. You're a good aunt too.

Love,

Trudi

• Make the reader feel that the gift is special to you by describing what you like about it.

Name
Address
City, State Zip

Date

Dear Louise,

I just left Jordan Makefield's office where I received a very enthusiastic pat on the back for an exceptionally well-run manager's meeting. Mr. Makefield said it was the finest such event in the company's 17 years.

I told him that you made the difference, and that I've never before had an assistant who paid such loving attention to detail. You did us both proud, Louise. I'm very appreciative of the work you put into this project. Thank you!

Sincerely,

Lars

- Recognition is a major reward, particularly for young people who have aspirations to grow within an organization. Praise is a powerful motivator.

- Send the thank you letter as soon as possible after the good job was completed. That's when it will have the greatest impact.

Name
Address
City, State Zip

Date

Dear Lucy,

There are times when I wonder how this department ever functioned without you. You've upgraded virtually every office function, and you've also brought a sense of professionalism and grace to what had been a tense atmosphere.

In the rush of the day, I may not always sound as appreciative as I should. So I hope the enclosed bonus check will help say it for me. Thank you for being such a positive influence in the workplace, and thank you for making it possible for all of us to do a better job.

Yours truly,

Jim

- Taking time out to tell someone they are noticed and appreciated is both thoughtful and rewarding.

- Tieing a letter of praise to a bonus check or pay increase doubles the effect.

Name
Address
City, State Zip

Date

Mr. Charles Miller
Bamco Industries
1180 Levering Ave.
Los Angeles, CA 90024

Dear Charlie,

I'd been warned that manufacturing management was conservative, but I had no idea they burned innovators at the stake. I never thought that advocating a change in procedure was heresy, but it's obvious that they do.

If you hadn't been at the Monday meeting, I wouldn't have stood a chance. And a procedural change that you apparently agree will save tens of thousands of dollars would never have seen the light of day.

Thanks for the support. I hope I can return the favor some day.

Sincerely,

Hank

- You earn points in business (and elsewhere) by taking the time to thank people who are supportive. A handshake is fine, but a handwritten (or typed) note means special recognition.

- Acknowledge that the proposal/presentation/project may not have succeeded without support.

Name
Address
City, State Zip

Date

Dear Cheryl,

I don't know whether to be pleased or disappointed that some people didn't even know I was out of work for a week. You did such a wonderful job filling in during my illness, everything just sailed along.

I'm not sure how you managed double duty so well, but I appreciate every minute you put into it. I'd like to express my heartfelt thanks over lunch one day next week. I'll call to see when it will be convenient for you.

Thanks for helping out in my absence.

Gratefully,

Rich

- Tell the reader you're aware how well things went in your absence.

- A tangible reward, such as lunch or dinner, is a nice way to make your "thanks" particularly meaningful.

Name
Address
City, State Zip

Date

Mr. Norbert Kershaw
Taunton Manufacturing Company
98 West Station Avenue
Erie, PA 16505

Dear Bert:

I got the account!

I can't imagine what you told Don Bryson about me, but he acted as if I were doing him a favor by showing up for the appointment. I've never made an easier sale.

I hope you know how grateful I am for the recommendation. Please be my guest for dinner next Thursday when I'm in town for a meeting. It's just a small way of saying thanks. I'll call on Monday to confirm.

This couldn't have come at a better time for me. It's tough for freelancers right now.

With much appreciation,

Kurt

• An enthusiastic response is a great reward for someone who has taken the time to make a recommendation.

• If the recommendation paid off, be sure to say so.

Thank You for Allowing Me to Use You as a Reference (13-41)

Name
Address
City, State Zip

Date

Mr. Alfred Tyrell
Pinelands National Bank
Poplar and Lawrence Streets
Elmont, KS 66608

Dear Mr. Tyrell:

I had an interview this morning that I felt was going very well.
When the interviewer—Harry Olin, of Great American Enterprises—asked for references and I gave your name, the interview
immediately progressed to the next level. Mr. Olin was very
impressed that you would "stand up" for me.

I won't know until next week if I have the job, but I do know how
much I appreciate your allowing me to use your name as a
reference. Thank you for your help.

Sincerely,

Ellis Burton

- Even if you can't offer an anecdote about how the use of the person's name was helpful, a simple "thank you" is mandatory.

- If someone is nice enough to allow you to use their name, make it a point to offer an occasional update on your job search.

Thank You for the Contribution (13-42)

Name
Address
City, State Zip

Date

Ms. Rita Lapham
Motor Homes of America, Inc.
3000 Route 255 West
Round Lake, MN 56167

Dear Ms. Lapham:

The contribution your company made to the Bobby Gallagher Memorial Fund was a godsend. First, you should be aware that it was the single largest gift we've ever received.

Second, I want you to know that the dollars have been earmarked to provide motorized wheelchairs to spinal cord injury victims.

As the administrator of the fund—and, more personally, as Bobby Gallagher's mother—I want to thank you so much for your touching and generous contribution.

With gratitude and appreciation,

Lenore Gallagher

• Always acknowledge a contribution of any size.

• If possible, indicate how the dollars will be spent.

Thank You for the Grant (13-43)

Name
Address
City, State Zip

Date

Mr. Warren Penney
President
National Tires & Accessories
58 E. Richmond Street
Lexington, KY 40577

Dear Mr. Penney:

I don't know who first said it, but your company embodies the sentiment: "We make a living by what we receive. We make a life by what we give."

Your creation of five annual $1,000 grants to college-bound seniors will help "make a life" for many deserving students who might otherwise have had to forego a higher education. NTA's strong sense of social responsibility marks it as a company that cares about the future of our country.

On behalf of the students who will benefit from your generosity, and for the faculty and staff of St. Mary's, thank you. Please express our gratitude to everyone involved in this wonderful decision.

Sincerely,

Lorna Tolan

- When you use a quote, make sure its connection to the point you're making is obvious.

- Explain the value of the grant or scholarship.

Name
Address
City, State Zip

Date

Mr. Douglas Engelson
Senior Vice President
Carlson Fabrication Company
4100 Glenside Avenue
Troy, IL 62294

Dear Mr. Engelson:

I'm excited that you've agreed to create an apprenticeship program. I think you'll find that this arrangement will pay immediate dividends: (1) It will give many young people an opportunity to learn a trade, and (2) You'll get first crack at what will be a potential new employee pool...with each student trained the way you like.

Speaking for myself and, I think, for nearly every other student at Madison County Vo-tech, thank you. This is a real boost to our program and our future.

Very truly yours,

Pauline Winslow

• Remind the company that the benefits of participation flow two ways.

• Indicate that the results of cooperation will have a widespread effect.

Thank You for Sponsoring Our Team (13-45)

Name
Address
City, State Zip

Date

Mr. Andrew Marley
President
Pacific Hardware
1019 West Kaole Street
Kahului, HI 96732

Dear Mr. Marley:

Thank you for sponsoring our team in the Kahului 10-12 year-old summer baseball league.

No matter what happens on the field this summer, Pacific Hardware is in first place with 25 very happy girls and boys (and their parents and coaches!). As soon as the uniforms arrive, I'll bring my son to model one for you.

The first game is Tuesday, July 6, at 7:00 p.m. We'd consider it an honor if you'd throw out the first ball.

Thanks again for your interest and support. We appreciate your contribution to Kahului's children.

Very truly yours,

Nicholas Papuloa

- Be sure a sponsor is made to feel involved and appreciated.
- Keep the sponsor notified of every event.

Name
Address
City, State Zip

Date

Mr. Kenneth Guiness
Atlantis Industries
2000 Bayside Boulevard
Tampa, FLA 33602

Dear Mr. Guiness:

Thanks to the fascinating presentation of your telecommunications specialist, Linda Giordano, everyone who attended our dinner feels like a communications expert. We were all enthralled by her discussion of how upcoming innovations will enable us to communicate more effectively in the future.

On behalf of the Tampa Area Small Business Association, I thank you for providing us with such a stimulating speaker. Many of our members have already expressed an interest in putting Atlantis systems to work for them.

Best Regards,

Marie-Elise Foreman

- Tell the reader how the audience responded to the speaker.

- Let the reader feel that their organization benefited by providing the speaker.

Requests for Information and Assistance 14

A simple request for information requires that you be brief and direct; a request for assistance requires more of an explanation. In either case, it must not seem as if you're making a demand. When your request is asking for effort or commitment on the reader's part, it should be tailored to their needs (Why should they contribute? What will be gained by participating?)

Education. When requesting information that could have a bearing on your future (student aid, scholarships, admissions, transfers), you need to do some homework. Are you sending your request to the right department? (If not, you run the risk of a delayed answer or no answer, either of which could have a negative impact.) Is there a deadline for submission? (Missing a cut-off date can have disastrous consequences.)

If you're trying to persuade an educator to do something for you, express your request in terms of the institution's goals. For example, if you want a dorm transfer, it should be because you feel it will positively affect your academic performance, not because your roommate likes country music and you prefer rock.

Organizations. When you're writing as a representative of a civic or charitable organization, don't assume the reader knows your organization and the work it performs. Whether you're asking for assistance or a contribution, answer the reader's basic question: "How will I benefit?" or "How will my contribution help someone?"

Institutions and agencies. Large companies, bureaucrats and politicians are besieged by letters, requests, suggestions and complaints every day. Although most do a good job of responding, the speed and quality of the response is largely based on the clarity of the initiating letter.

For example, if you want information about a congressperson's voting record or position on an important issue, don't offer a lengthy preamble about your feelings; just ask for the specific information. If there is data that identifies the subject of your letter, such as the name or number of a form, the name or number of a piece of legislation, or the location of the property in question, display that data prominently.

Senior citizens. Letters are links to the outside world, particularly if you have limited mobility or access. They can be effective in (1) obtaining necessary information, and (2) pressuring businesses and officials to pay attention to your specific needs.

There are record numbers of senior citizens today who can use their collective power to gain the attention and services they want and need. Focus your letter of request on a reason why a merchant, institution, or official should cater to you (e.g., gaining business, backing or votes).

Travel. Travel plans can be dramatically simplified if you state your requirements in writing, and request written recommendations and confirmations, as well. With a written record of what was said and quoted, there's little room for error. Ask for confirmation numbers, dates when information was given, and the names of people who supplied it. Then, if certain accommodations were promised in writing but weren't delivered, you'll have recourse.

Request for College Catalog and Application (14-01)

Name
Address
City, State Zip

Date

UCLA
Undergraduate Admissions
405 Hilgard Avenue
Los Angeles, CA 90024

Dear Sir or Madam:

I plan to enter college as a freshman in the Fall of 19XX.

Would you please send me a catalog and an application for admission?

Thank you.

Very truly yours,

Aurora Hidalgo

- There's no need to embroider a letter such as this. Simply ask for what you need.
- Specify when you plan to start college.

Request for College Interview (14-02)

Name
Address
City, State Zip

Date

Sharon Andrews
Dean of Admissions
Mount Holyoke College
College Street
South Hadley, MA 01075-1488

Dear Dean Andrews:

Now that I've applied to Mount Holyoke for the Class of 19XX, I'm anxious to share my goals with you in a personal interview.

I'm planning to visit the campus in February and I'd like to schedule a meeting for any Friday in that month.

Please let me know which date is most convenient for you.

I look forward to getting acquainted with you and with Mount Holyoke.

Sincerely,

Nicole D. Chung

- Convey an assertive attitude.

- Allow plenty of lead-time to schedule a mutually convenient date for the interview.

Inquiry About Scholarships and Loans (14-03)

Name
Address
City, State Zip

Date

Admissions Office
Pennsylvania State University
University Park, PA 16802

Dear Admissions Officer:

I would like to receive information on your scholarship and student loan programs.

I'm a National Honor Society junior with a special interest in drama. I'm impressed with the scope of Penn State's Theater Arts program, and hope that I will be able to participate in it.

I'm exploring ways of financing my education, and I look forward to learning what Penn State has to offer in this regard.

Thank you.

Ramona Clark

• Give the school some idea of your interests and achievements. There may be special scholarships available.

• State when you're planning to attend college.

Request for Reinstatement after Suspension (14-04)

Name
Address
City, State Zip

Date

Eugene M. Hoechst, Ed.D.
Dean of Men
Albert Thomas University
Lamp Post Lane and Hiller Road
Arlington Heights, IL 60005

Dear Dean Hoechst:

I appreciate the university's decision not to press charges for breaking and entering. When we decided to take your door off its hinges and run it up the flagpole on the ROTC grounds, we thought of it as a prank, not as a criminal act.

In the light of day, I understand the implications and consequences of my actions. I deeply regret my behavior, not just because I made a fool of myself and earned a suspension, but because I displayed such poor judgment.

I apologize for the concern and consternation I caused you and the university. I hope you'll consider a reinstatement for next semester. There will be no recurrence.

Thanks for your kindness and fairness. I look forward to the opportunity of redeeming myself.

Very truly yours,

Alexander Campbell

- Don't defend indefensible actions.

- By taking responsibility, you demonstrate the maturity that is required for forgiveness.

Request for Professor's Assistance (14-05)

Name
Address
City, State Zip

Date

James R. Worthy, Ph.D.
Whitman College
1240 Arnold Hall
Whitman, MA 02382

Dear Professor Worthy:

I'm in trouble, and I need your help.

I signed up for Astronomy 101 because (a) I need three science credits to complete my degree requirements, and (b) you have a reputation for bringing science to life. It never occurred to me, however, that a background in chemistry and physics would be helpful in understanding the material. As an Art & Architectural History major, I have neither.

I'm not afraid of hard work, and I'll do whatever's necessary to catch up. But I don't even know what I don't know. Perhaps you could direct me to some resources that would be helpful, or give me the name of a graduate assistant who can tutor me. I'll do whatever it takes.

Since I already enjoy the class, imagine how much more I'd like it if I really understood what you were talking about! I'll check with you after Friday's class.

Sincerely,

Gerold Pennock

- Asking for help always grabs the reader's attention.

- Be specific about the type of help you require.

Request for Dorm Transfer (14-06)

Name
Address
City, State Zip

Date

Dean Arthur Williams
Dean of Students
Center Valley College
Old Main Road
Lynnewood, WA 98037   Re: Request for Room Transfer

Dear Dean Williams:

My dorm adviser has told me that no mid-semester room transfers are permitted. So I'm appealing to you to make an exception.

Doing well in college means a lot to me. It's a struggle financially. I work for my meals at the Student Union Building and tutor local high school students in math.

I hope that conveys the idea that I'm serious about my responsibilities. My roommate may be serious, too, but not in a compatible way. For example, he studies with loud music in the background; I need quiet. He doesn't mind constant interruptions from his friends; I can't handle breaks in my concentration. He doesn't seem to need sleep; I can't function without it.

Will you please authorize my transfer to another dorm, or at least to another room in this dorm? I would appreciate your help. I'll move <u>anywhere</u> to find a more compatible roommate. My dorm phone is 555-3382.

Sincerely,

Peter Benning

• Headline the request to get the attention of the reader.

• Back up your request with factual information.

Letter to Board of Education Regarding Bad Teacher (14-07)

Name
Address
City, State Zip

Date

Ms. Sylvia E. Finegold
Chairperson
Region 2 Board of Education
6056 York Road
Bloomington, IN 47402

Dear Ms. Finegold:

How would you respond if you were in the fourth grade and your teacher just told you that the question you asked was the stupidest question she'd ever heard? If you're anything like my son, you'd respond by withdrawing emotionally, and falling behind in your schoolwork because you'd be afraid to ask another question.

It took two months of counselling to discover why my son's attitude toward school had changed so dramatically. But the teacher (Mrs. Camilla Swilling) and the administration of the Elverson Elementary School are unwilling to discuss the issue. So that puts it squarely in your lap.

What action will you take against a teacher who demonstrates an astonishing lack of understanding and sensitivity to young children? How will you protect the 22 children in her classroom? What steps will you take to try to undo the damage she's wreaked on my son?

I'll expect an answer within the week.

Very truly yours,

Arlene Steckman

• An emotional appeal is warranted in situations like this.

• Asking direct questions tells the reader you expect a response.

Name
Address
City, State Zip

Date

Mrs. Roslyn Nathanson
1 Skylark Lane
Annapolis, MD 21403

Dear Mrs. Nathanson:

One hour of your time could bring months of relief to hundreds of starving children. That's why I'm appealing to you for help.

Eight years ago I was privileged to accompany GLOBALERT officials on a world-wide fact-finding mission. The devastation and despair that I witnessed remain with me to this day.

Upon my return to the U.S., I vowed to dedicate myself to freeing the children of the world from starvation. Today I'm the regional representative for GLOBALERT.

We are making a difference, but there are so many hungry children! Will you join the fight and take a few moments to canvass your neighborhood for tax-deductible contributions?

Together we can weave a tapestry of hope that will nourish starving children into the next millenium.

Thank you.

Gratefully,

Shirlee W. Smith

- Appeal to the reader's compassion by stating the urgency of the cause.

- Let the reader know how their help can make a difference.

Would You Offer Items for Charity Auction? (14-09)

Name
Address
City, State Zip

Date

Mr. Arvin Peterson
226 Elsinore Drive
Minneapolis, MN 55450

Dear Mr. Peterson:

As a highly acclaimed author and illustrator who resides in Minneapolis, you have a high profile. You draw crowds.

As chairperson of the Hahnemann Heart Hospital charity auction, I'm hoping to draw crowds to our celebrity event on February 18 at the Four Seasons Hotel. Will you help?

Would you be willing to donate a personal item or service for sale to the highest bidder? An autographed first edition of one of your books, a tour of your studio—whatever you decide. I'm confident that any item with the name "Arvin Peterson" attached to it will set off a frenzy of bidding and generate needed revenue for the hospital.

Hahnemann Heart Hospital is the leading cardiac facility in the Great Lakes region. With help from celebrities like yourself, we can grow even stronger.

I'll call you next week to find out what you'd like to put on the auction block.

Sincerely,

Patricia Astair

• Give the reader some flexibility regarding the type of donation they might make.

• Stress the importance of the reader's participation.

Name
Address
City, State Zip

Date

Emmett Evergast
WWDB FM
Carmel Square
Santa Barbara, CA 93107

Dear Mr. Evergast:

Congratulations on your recent ratings triumph. I'm not surprised that "Plant World" dominates the radio airwaves. Southern California would turn brown and wilt without your daily doses of gardening advice.

The Santa Barbara Arboretum would be honored if you would act as honorary chairperson for our annual "Flora Extravaganza" to be held at the Arboretum on May 6-8. As you know, this event is Santa Barbara's pride, and it draws more than 10,000 visitors each year. The enclosed brochure should answer any questions you might have.

Although we'd love for you to be actively involved, we'd be more than grateful if you would just give us permission to use your name and photo on our program and advertising materials. We'd also like to honor you at a preview reception for media and invited guests on March 5 at 6:00 p.m. at the Arboretum.

Your name and our event seem to be a perfect match. I hope you'll honor us with your participation.

Sincerely,

Rosamond Braun
Event Coordinator

- Express your regard for the reader and your reasons for making the request.

- High-profile people have busy schedules. Be candid about the amount of time the honorary role will require.

Offer to Volunteer My Services (14-11)

Name
Address
City, State Zip

Date

Volunteer Services
Abington Memorial Hospital
4 Hilldale Parkway
Vancouver, WA 98668

Dear Sir or Madam:

I'd like to offer my services as a volunteer. I'm available Tuesday or Thursday afternoons from noon to 4:00 P.M., and one Sunday afternoon per month.

I'd love to share my gift for storytelling and reading with the children on the pediatric floor. Ideally, I'd like to establish a regular weekly story hour in the children's lounge.

If you can't use my help in pediatrics, I'd be happy to deliver books and magazines to patients via the hospital mobile library.

I realize that it may not be possible to accommodate my specific requests. I ask only that I not be assigned to the Critical Care area.

I look forward to joining the Abington Memorial Hospital volunteer staff. I'll call your office in a few days to arrange an introductory meeting.

Very truly yours,

Edith Blanchard

- Be specific about your availability and areas of interest.
- If you feel you would be uncomfortable working in a certain area or doing a certain task, say so.

Name
Address
City, State Zip

Date

Dear Neighbor,

Would you like to see the vacant lot on Downing Street turned into a playground? And a traffic light installed at the intersection of Lawton and Park before someone is killed? Perhaps you'd sleep better if a Neighborhood Watch Team were patrolling the streets. And maybe you'd enjoy seeing trees line the sidewalks, adding beauty and shade to the area.

Too good to be true? Not if we all join forces. Not if you meet with your neighbors—on Tuesday, May 22, at 7:00 p.m.—to form an action committee. Jane Redpath, of nearby Mt. Airy Street, is going to tell us how she and her neighbors accomplished similar "miracles" in their section of town...and how we can do the same.

There really is strength in numbers. Together, we can add to the quality of life in our neighborhood. Join us for coffee and cake at my home next Tuesday (address above), and help us launch the Oak Lane Action Committee! We're going to make this neighborhood better for our families.

If you have any questions about the meeting, please feel free to call me at 555-6329. And before you put this letter away, mark your calendar! I'll see you on the 22nd.

Your neighbor,

Sally Burke

- No matter how strongly you feel about a project, you must be able to convey your vision to others...and they must feel that there's something in it for them.

- Spell out all the important details about the meeting, even mentioning if refreshments will be served.

Name
Address
City, State Zip

Date

Dear Sandy and Jules,

Wouldn't it be wonderful to have musical concerts in our community, instead of having to drive 30 miles into St. Louis? And wouldn't it be terrific to have regular "issues" discussions, with speakers such as State Senator Trevor Hauseman and noted psychologist Dr. Zora Winkowski? I know how much that appeals to you. And you can help us make it happen.

As you know, I've been very active in the Allentown Civic Association, and I'm proud of many of the things we've done to improve the quality of life in the community. But to create some of the activities and events we have in mind, we need the help of committed people like yourselves.

I'm extending a personal invitation to you. Will you join us for a "get to know you" meeting on Wednesday, March 12, at 7:00 p.m., at my home? You'll have the chance to meet many of your neighbors, to hear the plans we've made to upgrade the cultural life of our community...and to learn the role you can play in helping us do it.

It would be great if you could join us. And I think you'd enjoy being a part of the group. I'll call to confirm your attendance.

Sincerely,

Emil Valerian

- A personalized letter to prospective members is far more effective than a form letter.

- If possible, customize the letter for each recipient. For example, if music is important to the reader, talk about planned concerts.

Name
Address
City, State Zip

Date

Ms. Harriet Markey, R.N.
2114 Rossner Drive
Lincoln, NE 68501

Dear Ms. Markey:

I was impressed with the recent article in the Lincoln Times describing your work with victims of sexual abuse. The article illustrated how compassion and experience combine to ease the trauma of rape victims as they pass through your emergency room.

I've just been named Director of the newly established Crime Victims Center. We're a support group, counseling service, and follow-up facility for victims of sexual abuse.

Our volunteer counselors and staff would benefit enormously from your experience and expertise. Would you be available to speak at our monthly meeting on Thursday, May 13 at 7:00 p.m. at the Center? We'd like to allow about an hour and a half for your remarks and follow-up questions.

Our goal at the Crime Victims Center is to restore dignity and self-respect to victims of sexual abuse. We would greatly appreciate your participation.

I'll call you next week to see if you'll be available on May 13.

Sincerely,

Merle Valentine

- Give the reader an idea of who the audience will be.

- Be specific about time, date, location, topic and length of speech.

Name
Address
City, State Zip

Date

Ms. Winifred Alsop
Institute for Arts Enrichment
1000 Boulevard of the Arts
Cleveland, OH 44101

Dear Winifred:

Five years ago, you conceived a plan for an arts education program to enrich the lives of school children all over the Cleveland area. Today the Institute for Arts Enrichment has reached tens of thousands of youngsters—and is still growing. You have my respect and admiration. As one of the original board members, I'm proud to have played a role in launching such a worthwhile project.

Now that the Institute has "grown up," I feel it's time for me to step aside as Secretary. You need fresh energy and new ideas, and I've become distracted by other commitments.

Please accept my resignation as Secretary and board member effective the date of our next board meeting. Also, please accept my gratitude. It was a privilege to work with you.

Very truly yours,

Alison R. Farmer

• Praising the work of the organization should help offset any antagonism that your resignation might cause.

• Be sure to state the date when your resignation becomes effective.

Name
Address
City, State Zip

Date

Public Affairs Department
Continental Landfill, Inc.
One Warrington Plaza
Staten Island, NY 10303

Dear Sir or Madam:

Please send a copy of your current annual report and any other information that may help me evaluate your company for future stock purchases.

Sincerely,

Sterling Wilcox

- Most public corporations will gladly honor a request for financial data.

- If you ask only for the annual report, that's what you'll get. An expanded request may deliver additional information that will help you determine the character and investment potential of a company.

Name
Address
City, State Zip

Date

Mr. Allen Driscoll
University Hospital Research Center
1224 Weymouth Station
Casper, WY 82608

Dear Mr. Driscoll:

I received a solicitation, under your name, for a contribution to help fund an expansion of your facility.

Before I consider writing a check, I need to know your position on animal rights in research. In other words, (1) do you use animals and, if so, (2) how are their rights protected, and (3) what sorts of experiments are routinely conducted?

My support is based on your answer.

Very truly yours,

Lester Townsend

• Ask for whatever information you desire. There is no reason to hide your motive.

• If an action of yours depends upon the response, say so.

```
                          Name
                          Address
                       City, State Zip

Date

The Honorable Drew B. Richter
Senate Office Building
Washington, D.C. 20510

Dear Senator Richter:

I read in the March 15 issue of Time Magazine that you are
sponsoring a bill to freeze immigration into the United States.  If
enacted, such a law would affect members of my family who are
hoping to come to this country and ultimately to become citizens.

Would you please send me a copy of the bill and tell me your
justification for proposing it?

Very truly yours,


Ida T. Chin
```

- If you know which congressperson is sponsoring the bill, write directly to them.

- Identify the bill as specifically as you can. (If you know the number of the bill, include it.)

Request to Consumer Product Safety Commission (14-19)

Name
Address
City, State Zip

Date

Office of Public Affairs
Consumer Product Safety Commission
5401 Bard Avenue
Bethesda, MD 20816

Dear Sir or Madam:

Has there been a recall on the "Babykins" doll manufactured by Tidy Tot? I saw part of a news story about it on TV last night and I am concerned.

To avoid risk, I've taken the doll away from my two-year old. However, her refusal to eat or sleep without it is upsetting the household. If the doll is safe, I want to return it to my daughter as soon as possible.

Please rush whatever information you have about the "Babykins" doll. I'd appreciate being added to your mailing list so I can receive information on hazardous toys.

Thank you,

Irene Maxfield

- To avoid unnecessary confusion and delay, make sure you send your inquiry to the appropriate government agency.

- Save yourself from having to write another letter like this by asking to be on the mailing list.

Name
Address
City, State Zip

Date

Consumer Product Information
Ariad Pharmaceuticals, Inc.
1100 Loeffler Street
Akron, OH 44307   Re: Benzodiazepine

Dear Sir or Madam:

I read an article that listed you as one of the manufacturers of an anti-insomnia drug known as benzodiazepine. I'm planning to visit a physician for treatment of insomnia, and I'd like to discuss this very promising drug with him.

Please send whatever literature is available, including data on potential side effects, non-compatible medicines, food or beverages to avoid, etc. Thanks for your prompt attention.

Sincerely,

Victor Olinski

- You may be bringing your physician information that is new to them.

- Highlight the name of the product you're inquiring about to help the reader to assist you more quickly.

Letter to Tax Assessor about Real Estate Tax (14-21)

Name
Address
City, State Zip

Date

Town Assessor
Calhoun Municipal Building
2900 Mercer Street
Clarksdale, MS 38614   Re: Lot 515, Baldwin Hill

Dear Sir or Madam:

After checking on the assessment of neighbors' homes which are comparable to mine, it's apparent that the township has erred in its assessment of my property.

For example, the neighbor to my left (a corner lot) was assessed at $3,211—nearly $900 less than my assessment. The neighbor to the right was assessed at $3,062—more than $1,000 less than mine.

We should be able to work this out without going through the formal appeals process. My guess is that a clerk made a calculation error, or the assessor made a series of mistakes in identifying improvements.

Would you please review my records, then call me at 555-8374. I'd like to resolve this promptly.

Sincerely,

Adam Shochet

- Demonstrate that you've done your homework, in this case "comparison shopping."

- Offer some reasons as to how the error could have been made, and ask for a review.

Letter to Police Chief Requesting Neighborhood Patrol (14-22)

Name
Address
City, State Zip

Date

Chief Parker Lebeau
Bakersfield Police
3218 Hinkley Road
Bakersfield, CA 93308

Dear Chief Lebeau:

During the past few weeks, our neighborhood has been repeatedly awakened in the early morning hours by the sounds of blaring rock music, crashing beer bottles, and screamed obscenities. A far more serious problem has accompanied these incidents: There's been a dramatic increase in vandalism. Garages have been spray-painted with graffiti, shrubs and flowers have been up-rooted, and windows have been broken.

We need a more visible police presence. None of the incidents occurred during neighborhood watch patrols, so it seems reasonable to assume we can eliminate the problem if it's known that police are patrolling the neighborhood.

If you need more specific information, call me at 555-3920. I'll be more than happy to cooperate in any way. Thanks for your help.

Sincerely,

Cindy Corley

- Don't assume that other people are reporting a problem so you don't have to. Besides, the more pressure there is to perform, the better the results.

- Explain the incidents that led to your request.

Name
Address
City, State Zip

Date

Mr. Garth Whalen
New Sweden Public Schools
White Sulphur Road
New Sweden, ME 04762

Dear Mr. Whalen:

You've constantly reminded the community to have our children ready to board when the school bus arrives each morning. I'd like to make a similarly reasonable request: Please have the bus arrive on schedule.

It's wrong to make the kids wait 20-30 minutes beyond their scheduled pick-up times. They get rambunctious, they run over people's lawns, they dart into the street, and they're taught that there's no need to be prompt.

Speaking for the parents whose children take bus #39 each day, I'd like your assurance that the bus will show up on time...or that the schedule will reflect a more realistic arrival time. You can write to the address above, or call me at 555-4391.

Don't you agree that for the children's well-being this should be resolved as quickly as possible? I'll expect an answer by Friday, February 2.

Sincerely,

Harry Hopkins

- Let the reader know that a "contract" is a two-way street.

- Don't make your complaint personal; the children are the issue.

Name
Address
City, State Zip

Date

Ms. Anne Marie Tartaglione
Chief Engineer
Mount Carmel Sewer Department
5320 Perina Boulevard
Mount Carmel, AL 35740

Dear Ms. Tartaglione:

Six weeks have passed since I reported that sewage smells were leaking from the town's septic tanks, 300 feet behind my home. While there's been a flurry of activity since then, the odor has become more oppressive.

Although you've assured me that the gas is non-toxic, you haven't supplied any test results or scientific data. I'm not willing to wait any longer.

Since I'm being treated as a bother, rather than as a taxpayer, I'm turning this problem over to my attorney. She'll be in touch.

With concern,

Lonette Berry

cc: Mayor Eldon Briggs

- When dealing with an unresponsive or incapable municipal department, create a written record. Always follow up phone conversations with letters. They have more legal weight.

- Send copies of the correspondence to higher local, county and state officials.

Letter to Zoning Commission Requesting Variance (14-25)

Name
Address
City, State Zip

Date

Zoning Board
Jordan Township Municipal Building
1100 Mercer Street   Re: Variance Request
Jordan, IL 61081   Lot 515A, Block 23

Dear Sir or Madam:

The enclosed plans for a building addition fall well within the
township's structural requirements. Although the positioning of
the "mother-in-law suite" brings it one foot closer to my neighbor's
property line than township regulations currently allow, my
neighbor has no objection to the construction (copy of letter
enclosed).

I think you'll agree that the structure is consistent with the
architecture that's prevalent in the neighborhood. And the builder,
DeMartini Brothers, has a well-deserved reputation for excellence.
I'm assured that the suite will appear to have always been a part
of our house.

Since the only person even remotely affected by this request has
approved the variance, I trust you will, too. If there is no need for
a hearing, please send the necessary work permits to me in the
enclosed self-addressed, postage-paid reply envelope.

Sincerely,

Howard Cox

- If you don't ask for something, you'll never get it. There are always exceptions to
  rules.

- Document your requests to save time and energy.

Letter to Jury Selection Board Requesting Postponement (14-26)

Name
Address
City, State Zip

Date

Jury Selection Board
Hermiker County
5322 Racine Avenue
Little Falls, NY 13365

Dear Sir or Madam:

While I believe that jury duty is a solemn responsibility, I respectfully request that my selection be deferred to a later date.

During the dates in question, I will be in the middle of intense labor negotiations that will affect the well-being of hundreds of employees. I've put months of preparation into these upcoming meetings, and it would be impossible for my union to replace me at this point.

I would be more than happy to fulfill my obligations to the community at a later date. But it would cause an extreme hardship to many people if I had to serve at this time.

Thank you for your consideration.

Respectfully,

Sean Lyons

- Use a respectful tone, and indicate your belief in the system.

- Explain the specific circumstance that you feel should cause the board to reschedule you.

Name
Address
City, State Zip

Date

Mr. Leonard White
Circle Diner
522 Route 686
Westminster, CO 80020

Dear Mr. White:

Because you combine fine food with moderate pricing, you enjoy the patronage of many of the area's senior citizens. In fact, I can't remember ever coming for dinner when there wasn't a wait for a table. However, you're losing customers because there's no seating in the waiting area.

It's tough enough to get up the stairs to your entrance. Standing during a 20- to 30-minute wait once we get there is more than many of us can handle. If you would simply place a few benches in the entryway, you'd be (1) telling your regular customers that you appreciate and respect them, and (2) increasing your business because most of your lost diners would return. Favorable word of mouth would generate new customers, as well.

A little bit of TLC with seniors, Mr. White, will pay off in a big way. May I have a response?

Sincerely,

May Gooden

• A good suggestion letter benefits the sender and the receiver.

• By asking for a response, the reader knows you are expecting action.

Name
Address
City, State Zip

Date

Mr. Abner Sherman
Village Pharmacy
Crown Plaza Center
Van Nuys, CA 91405

Dear Mr. Sherman:

Do you know why my daughter buys my various pharmaceuticals in her neighborhood and brings them to me on weekends? Because I have no way of getting them myself. You're only a half-mile from my apartment, but I can't drive (bad eyesight), can't walk that far (arthritis), and you don't deliver.

If you multiply my circumstances by that of only 100 senior citizens in the area (and there are a lot more than that!), my guess is that you're losing at least $5,000-$10,000 in business each month. Seniors buy lots of pills! Since it would probably cost you no more than $600-$800 a month for a part-time deliveryperson, it seems to me that you're cheating yourself out of a lot of business.

The minute you offer a delivery service—even if there's a small charge—I'll start to use your drug store. You'll dramatically increase your revenues, and I'll give my daughter a break. That would help everybody!

Sincerely,

Wes Odums

• Telling your personal problems can help to make a strong case.

• Money talks! Use increased income as an incentive.

Request to Bus Company for Senior Discount Information (14-29)

Name
Address
City, State Zip

Date

Senior Citizen Fare Information
Northwest Transportation Company
1100 E. Wyoming Avenue
Spokane, WA 99254

To Whom It May Concern:

I'd like to take advantage of your senior citizens fare discount.
Would you please send me information describing:

> Hours the fare is in effect
> Routes covered
> Discounted fare
> How fare is paid (e.g., cash when I ride, or do I need to
>   obtain tokens in advance?)
> Identification required.

I appreciate your help.

Sincerely,

Michael Esterhaus

- Don't miss out on an age "perk" simply because you're not sure of cost, procedure, availability, etc. Most organizations have literature readily available to answer all your questions.

- State exactly what information you need.

Name
Address
City, State Zip

Date

Medicare Disbursement Office
1222 Robbins Street
San Francisco, CA 94123   Re: Claim# 10239A53

Dear Sir or Madam:

I recently had cataract surgery, and was given dark glasses to wear for a period of time after the surgery. According to my physician, Medicare is supposed to pay for the glasses, as well as the surgery. However, payment for the glasses has been denied, apparently in error.

Would you please recheck your paperwork? I'm certain the glasses are covered, and I'd like your confirmation that the bill has been paid.

Sincerely,

Mildred Tanner

• When questioning a claim, put the claim number in a prominent place.

• Ask that a confirmation of payment be sent to you.

Notification to Social Security Administration of Death of Spouse (14-31)

Name
Address
City, State Zip

Date

Social Security Administration
2600 Mt. Ephraim Avenue
Camden, NJ 08104   Re: SS# 157-62-7002

To Whom It May Concern:

My husband, Ronald Morley, passed away on March 22, 19XX, at the age of 68. A copy of the death certificate has been forwarded to you by the Smith-Hardy Funeral Home.

Will you please send a copy of your publication, Survivors (05-10084), to help me understand death benefits and procedures? Thank you for your help.

Sincerely,

Edith Morley

- Normally, funeral directors forward copies of death certificates to their local SSA office. However, you should check with the funeral parlor to be sure.

- Include the deceased's social security number, as well as your own, to make it easier for SSA personnel to help you.

Request to Social Security Administration for Benefits Report (14-32)

Name
Address
City, State Zip

Date

Social Security Administration
131 West Street
Danbury, CT 06810

To Whom It May Concern:

Please send me a copy of <u>Request for Earnings and Benefit Estimate Statement</u> at the address listed above.

Sincerely,

Leandra Thomas

- In response to this letter, the SSA will send a form for you to complete that will help them project your retirement benefits. The entire process will take about six weeks.

- Don't clutter the letter with information about your retirement. It's a waste of your time and can distract from your request.

Request to Travel Agency for Estimate of Travel Costs (14-33)

Name
Address
City, State Zip

Date

Mr. Chad Davis
Travel Makers, Inc.
Allerton Plaza
Hollywood, SC 29449

Dear Mr. Davis:

After spending many enjoyable hours reading through the literature you provided about Las Vegas, we've decided on the trip we'd like to take. Here are the pertinent details:

1. Two adults.
2. 10 days, including travel time, from Saturday, June 12, through Monday, June 21.
3. Add a side trip to the Grand Canyon. Does it make sense to spend four days in Las Vegas, three in the Grand Canyon area (we'll need a mid-size rental car), and then three more in Vegas? I assume it's less expensive to fly home from Las Vegas?
4. Fly coach.
5. Stay in first-class hotels (we prefer a king or queen-size bed).

If you need any other information, call me during the day at (803) 555-7799, or in the evening at (803) 555-0247. Once you've determined available dates and costs, please give me a call and we'll meet to finalize our vacation schedule. Thanks so much for your help.

Cordially,

Elysse Potter

• Providing information via letter (or fax) helps insure that there will be no miscommunication.

• By listing the points that are important to you, there's less likelihood that the reader will miss anything.

Request for Confirmation of Travel Costs (14-34)

Name
Address
City, State Zip

Date

Mr. Jules Brentwood
Brentwood Travel
92 Parker Place
Parkersburg, WV 26103

Dear Jules:

We're inches away from giving you a deposit on the Italy-Switzerland-France tour you've recommended. But we can afford this trip only if we aren't hit with a lot of extras. So help us be certain there are NO surprises.

We need answers to the following questions. Does the price you gave us ($2,221 each) include:

	Yes	No	Add Extra $$$
All air and ground fares	___	___	$_____
All hotel rooms	___	___	$_____
All meals	___	___	$_____
All taxes/tips	___	___	$_____
All tour guides/attractions	___	___	$_____
Anything else	___	___	$_____

We need to work from a set budget, and we need your help to stay within it. The sooner we have your answer, the sooner you'll be able to book our space.

Thanks for your help and your patience.

Sincerely,

Vicki and Frank Mulholland

- Even people who specialize in a particular field make errors of omission. Identify your concerns line by line.

- Make it clear that no money will be paid until you have complete information.

Request to Travel Agency for Travel Information (14-35)

Name
Address
City, State Zip

Date

Landmark Travel, Inc.
246 Ramblewood Parkway
Laverock, PA 19075

Dear Sir or Madam:

My husband and I are planning to take a two-week vacation in mid-July. We want to do an in-depth tour (as much as possible within two weeks) of Italy. We're open to suggestions as to type of travel (e.g., air or boat), tour or independent, itinerary, etc. Here are our requirements:

1. We want to stay in deluxe hotels.
2. We prefer to visit locations that are rich in art and architecture.
3. Even though we plan to travel in July, we want to avoid the crowds as much as possible.
4. We're willing to spend up to $6,000 total for a first class trip.

Please send brochures, recommendations and any other descriptive material that will help us make a decision. If you need more information, please call me at (215) 555-5832.

Very truly yours,

Hilda Sloan

- The more specific your request, the better information you'll receive.

- Don't be afraid to indicate how much you're willing to pay. It will help the travel agent zero in on the best choices for you.

Confirmation of Reservation (14-36)

Name
Address
City, State Zip

Date

Reservations Manager
Lanai Majestic Hotel
Paradise Drive
Honolulu, HI 96815

Dear Sir or Madam:

I'd like to confirm a reservation made by phone earlier today for your eight-day "Island Paradise" package plan. According to your brochure, this plan includes the following:

o 7 nights at the Lanai Majestic, oceanfront room, king size bed, double occupancy.

o Full breakfast daily

o Island helicopter tour

o Honolulu and Pearl Harbor tour

Total cost of the package for two is $1,650.00 plus tax and gratuities.

Please send written confirmation of our reservations.

We look forward to our stay at the Lanai Majestic.

Very truly yours,

Mrs. Alvin J. Foreman

- Don't leave out any important details in your confirmation (e.g., oceanfront room, dietary restrictions, type of bed, etc.)

- Request written confirmation.

Cancellation of Reservation (14-37)

Name
Address
City, State Zip

Date

Ms. Gail Pritzker
Logan Travel Services
1010 Covina Street
Troy, MI 49309

Dear Gail:

Once, when I was younger, my boss listened to me complain endlessly about something that had gone wrong at work. And then he said, "Adversity can't do you in, it can only reveal your spirit."

I hope that has as much meaning for you as it did for me, because I'm about to test _your_ spirit. There's been a shake-up in my company, and all vacation plans have been put on hold. That means we have to cancel our European trip. I apologize for all the time and effort you put into finding us super rates and top accommodations.

Mary Ann and I are hoping that things will settle down quickly and we'll be able to resume our vacation plans. Even though we can't make the trip now, perhaps all the research you did on our behalf will still be applicable in the future.

I'd appreciate it if you would fax cancellation confirmations to my office as soon as possible at (313) 555-1828. Thanks for everything.

Sincerely,

Martin Bream

- If someone has worked hard on your behalf, and especially if they are only paid via commission on a completed sale, it's thoughtful to tell them how much their effort is appreciated.

- Always ask for cancellation confirmations or you may end up paying for a trip you never got to take.

Name
Address
City, State Zip

Date

County Clerk of Passport
Municipal Building
City of Virginia Beach
60 W. Woodbury Avenue
Virginia Beach, VA 23462

Dear Sir or Madam:

Please send me an application for a passport, along with any guidelines and specifications for material I'll need to obtain a passport.

Since I have to go out of the country in less than two months, I'd appreciate your prompt response.

Thank you.

Sincerely,

James Makita

- Since you need items such as an official birth certificate (not a copy) and a passport photo, and because it requires 2-4 weeks to process an application (and possibly longer during peak travel times), be certain to start in plenty of time or you may, literally, miss the boat.

- Visit your local county passport office to pick up an application and start the ball rolling if time is a factor.

Name
Address
City, State Zip

Date

Ms. Toni Bateman
Avalon Travel Agency
1112 Sixth Street
Fargo, ND 58102

Dear Toni:

Please send us guidelines on whatever health precautions are necessary during our upcoming trip to Central America. We've received so much advice (much of it contradictory), we'd appreciate whatever "official" information you can provide.

This is a much-anticipated trip for us, and we're anxious that nothing we sip, swallow, touch, or breathe interferes with our ambitious travel schedule. We appreciate the help (and patience) you've provided on every detail.

Sincerely,

Peter Agosto

- Make your request in the first sentence.

- Express some of your concerns to be certain that you get the correct information.

Sensitive Issues 15

Sensitive issues can be explosive if they're not handled with tact, diplomacy and a regard for the reader's feelings, as well as your own. A thoughtfully composed letter will help you avoid miscommunication while putting your desires, convictions and expectations "on the record." Just be certain that you write what you mean and you mean what you write. Once on paper, there's no guarantee your feelings will remain private. Be careful what you say and to whom you say it.

Love letters. A "love" or relationship letter is the most personal letter you can write. It takes courage to tell someone how much they mean to you. But if you don't do it, you may never know if your feelings are reciprocated. On the other hand, if your intention is to *extricate* yourself from a relationship, be considerate of the reader's feelings. Explain your decision and be firm. Vacillating only confuses the other person and prolongs an inevitable breakup.

Telling it like it is. If you've arrived at a point where you're ready to "tell it like it is," you might be so fed up with a situation or an individual that you don't care if your letter ends the relationship. As long as you recognize that possibility and are comfortable with it, go ahead and say whatever's on your mind. Describe how the reader's action (or inaction) is affecting you. State what you want from the reader, and tell what will happen if they fail to respond.

You hurt my feelings. This kind of letter shouldn't be about blame or laying a guilt trip on the reader. It should be about *you and your feelings*. Phrases like, "I felt sad (angry, scared, etc.) when you..." help to explain, in a nonjudgmental way, how the reader's actions affected you. When you talk about the person's unacceptable behavior, rather than the person as a whole, the relationship can be salvaged.

Saying no. The "saying no" letter might have the same repercussions as the "telling it like it is" letter—it could end the relationship. To avoid second thoughts or regrets, be absolutely certain that you're comfortable with your position before saying "no." List reasons for your negative response. Once you put your refusal on record, make it clear that your decision is final.

Name
Address
City, State Zip

Date

Dear Anne-Marie,

As you know, it isn't easy for me to express my feelings. My discomfort with emotion has been frustrating for both of us. Since I'm not a great verbal communicator, I've decided to write to you.

Lately I've felt a distance growing between us, and I realize that I'm responsible for it. I admit that my mind has been elsewhere. I know it's painful to be with someone who's not really "there," and I don't want to hurt you. That's why I think we should stop seeing each other. You are a fantastic person, and you deserve 100% of your partner's attention.

I don't know where my restlessness will lead me. I do know that wherever it is, I'll think of you often.

Affectionately,

Dave

- Take responsibility for breaking up the relationship.
- Leave the reader with positive feelings about herself and about you.

Dear John Letter (15-02)

Name
Address
City, State Zip

Date

Dear Zach,

You've probably sensed a problem between us lately, and I owe you an explanation.

I've begun to realize that our relationship has been based mainly on our physical attraction for each other. Our priorities and interests are just not as compatible as I first thought.

I think you're a terrific person who will make a great partner for the right person. I suspect she'll come along very soon.

I'll always cherish the time we've spent together. Hopefully, we can remain friends.

Fondly,

Kristin

- Assume responsibility for your feelings and actions.

- Acknowledge the value of the relationship but be firm about your decision to end it.

Name
Address
City, State Zip

Date

Dear Wendell,

I said I wanted to be alone. I said I needed time to think. Well, I've been alone and I've had time to think.

My conclusion?

I think I don't want to be alone.

Missing you,

Melissa

- Be forthright about your feelings.

- Humor can help to make your point.

Name
Address
City, State Zip

Date

Dear Brandon,

When something makes me feel good, I like to repeat the experience.

Being with you made me feel great. Here's why:

    1) You're a good listener.

    2) You have a wacky sense of humor.

    3) You can whistle a Mozart concerto.

Let's get together again? Soon?

Fondly,

Brigitte

- Tell the reader what you like about them. Be specific.

- Be candid about your desire to pursue the relationship.

Name
Address
City, State Zip

Date

Dear Franco,

For years you've floated in and out of my thoughts. For the past few days you've been my only thought. Now I have an irresistible urge to write to you.

I've changed a lot since we last met. I'm sure you have, too. I'd love to bring you up to date.

Might I interest you in a little deja-vu?

Hopefully,

Paula

- Arouse the reader's curiosity (e.g., "I've changed a lot," "I'm involved in a fascinating project," etc.).

- Suggest that you'd like to meet.

Name
Address
City, State Zip

Date

Dear Janine,

Lately I've been thinking about a quote I read in college:

"Absence is to love as wind is to fire. If the flame is
weak, the wind will extinguish it. If the flame is strong,
the wind will help it grow."

Our separation has made my feelings for you even stronger than
before. I miss you, I love you, and I can't imagine a future without
you.

There's only one thing we can do. Will you marry me?

With all my love,

Ted

• Tell the reader what led to your proposal.

• Convince the reader that the only response possible is an affirmative one.

Name
Address
City, State Zip

Date

Dear Alan,

Just when I was wondering how and when I'd have a chance to see you, I was told that I'd be going to a trade show in Milwaukee next month (June 17-20)! I'm giving you as much notice as possible so you can reserve an evening or two for me. Your mom said you'd be finished with your round of treatments by then.

Instead of my usual written update on the comings and goings of our mutual friends (wait 'til you hear the lowdown on Beth and Marty!), I'll keep you in suspense so you'll have to see me when I'm in town.

While you're counting the days until I get there, here's something that will entertain you: Rent a video called <u>Success Song</u>. It's two hours of sheer joy. What a pleasant surprise; a low-budget movie that has more going for it than most $50 million productions.

And if you're looking for something with a little more weight to it, you can read all about the decline of morality in <u>America: Satan's Brew</u>. It's written by a theologian, but it reads better than most novels. It will give us plenty to talk about (not that we ever need help in that area!).

As soon as I'm given my hours and responsibilities for the show, I'll call you to work out the details. It will be wonderful to have the chance to see you.

With love,

Kate

• Don't focus on the person's illness in your correspondence. Write about the day-to-day occurrences that anyone would want to hear about.

• Avoid platitudes such as, "I just know you'll have a complete recovery."

Name
Address
City, State Zip

Date

Dear Artie,

Do you remember when we were younger, and we used to sit around and philosophize? One time, when we were debating religion, I asked if you believed in an afterlife. You said, "No, when you're dead, you're dead." So I asked if that meant you were an atheist, and you joked, "No, I don't believe in that, either."

I don't know how long either of us will be around, but I do know how many great times we've shared and how much I have enjoyed having you for a brother. Even when we disagreed, we always respected each other. I've always felt sorry for brothers who haven't had a relationship like ours.

I don't think I ever said these words to you, but it seems appropriate now, especially since we're both getting on in years: I love you. You've been a great friend as well as a great brother, and I cherish the time we've had together. Thanks for bringing so much to my life.

Your devoted brother,

Herbie

- Often people regret having unexpressed thoughts after a loved one is gone. A letter like this "sets the record straight," particularly for people who have difficulty verbalizing their thoughts.

- A shared vignette or two will bring a smile of recognition.

Name
Address
City, State Zip

Date

Carl,

On several occasions I've told you that your attentions aren't welcome. Yet you persist in telephoning me, lurking around my office, and following me.

I'm giving you notice that if this stalking doesn't cease <u>immediately</u>, I will notify the police. There are stalking laws in this state, and I will file charges.

Abigail Wharton

• Make the reader understand that you consider their behavior to be stalking. They may be surprised to hear this.

• State what you plan to do about it.

Name
Address
City, State Zip

Date

Mr. Jeremy Luff
3550 Alistair Avenue
Boston, MA 02167

Dear Mr. Luff:

Our daughter has repeatedly told you that her relationship with you is over, yet you continue to harass her. Your refusal to accept Michelle's decision is causing her mental anguish and disrupting her studies.

If you don't stop this threatening behavior immediately, we will notify the police. Our daughter's well-being is in jeopardy and we intend to safeguard it.

With great concern,

Andrew W. Smith

- Take a firm stand.

- State the consequences that will result if your demands aren't met.

Name
Address
City, State Zip

Date

Dear Penny,

You say that you want what's best for me. That's what I want, too. Unfortunately we don't agree on what "best" is.

I know you mean well when you tell me how to handle things, but I prefer to make my own decisions. While I welcome your friendship and support, I won't tolerate your interference.

Sincerely,

Lori

- It's important to sound sure of yourself when you're dealing with a meddler.
- State your terms for continuing the relationship.

Name
Address
City, State Zip

Date

Dear Kevin,

My intention in writing this letter isn't to hurt you. It's to end the
duplicity and the tension.

My relationship with Charlotte has developed beyond friendship.
It wasn't planned; it just happened.

We're in love with each other. That may seem incomprehensible
to you, but our feelings for each other have grown over time.

We realize the pain that this revelation will cause you. But it's
time for complete honesty. Charlotte and I can't keep our feelings
secret any more.

We don't expect your forgiveness, but we do hope for some level
of understanding.

Charlotte thought that if this news came to you in a letter, it would
give you a little time to digest the information before you and she
talked about it.

Sincerely,

Gil

- Be forthright about your own feelings and your intentions.

- Explain why you're delivering this news in a letter.

Name
Address
City, State Zip

Date

Ms. Sudmeyer:

Actions have consequences. The consequences of your association with my husband have been pain and embarrassment for my
family.

If you don't end this adulterous relationship, <u>you</u> will be the one
who suffers consequences.

    1) I will tell your husband.
    2) I will go to your office and tell your boss and co-workers.
    3) I will post a notice on your church bulletin board describing
       your behavior.
    4) I will take additional action without prior warning.

My husband has acknowledged his responsibility in this affair and
has expressed his intention to end it. Do not write to him,
telephone him or try to see him.

Adamantly,

Katherine Arnold

- State your demands.

- Explain what you'll do if they aren't met.

Name
Address
City, State Zip

Date

Dear Lillian,

People often comment on the peaceful atmosphere of my home. I think the harmony exists because of my family's commitment to tolerance, flexibility and humor.

I expect the same from my guests. That's why I was stunned by the racist remarks you made here last weekend. Your comments upset the other guests and ruined my dinner party.

Your attitude is inconsistent with everything we believe in. Given the circumstances, you won't be invited again.

Regretfully,

Betty

- Tell the reader why the behavior was offensive to you.

- Leave no doubt in the reader's mind about future social interaction with you.

You Have a Problem with Alcohol (15-15)

Name
Address
City, State Zip

Date

Dear Stuart,

Writing this letter could cost me your friendship, but I care enough about you to take the risk.

I'm concerned about your drinking. Take an honest look at your repeated absences from work, your constant money problems, and your history of DWI's and accidents. They are all alcohol related.

Out of concern for you, I've done some research on the subject. I've even started attending Al-Anon meetings. I hope you'll let me share what I've learned.

You are a valuable human being. I'd like to help you. Please let me—for both our sakes.

Fondly,

Toni

• Tell the reader why you think they have a problem with alcohol. Don't be judgmental.

• Stress your desire to help.

Name
Address
City, State Zip

Date

Dear Gene,

Up until a few months ago, I thought we had been succeeding at keeping any animosity from our divorce under wraps. We've both been better off for it, and the kids have certainly benefitted from the lack of sniping and confrontation. So it doesn't make sense that your child support payments have suddenly stopped coming.

School starts in less than two weeks and that means the kids need some new clothes, school supplies and lunch money. Without your payments, I can't even buy the bare essentials.

If I don't have at least two payments by next Friday, Gene, I'll have to ask my lawyer to notify the court. Please help me avoid a step neither of us wants to take.

Sincerely,

Lisa

- Avoid statements that blame the other party. They only cause anger and resentment.

- By asking someone to help you avoid taking unpleasant action, you demonstrate that both of you will benefit.

You're a Bigot (15-17)

Name
Address
City, State Zip

Date

Dear Lance,

You're a puzzle to me. You always seem to function well in multi-racial, multi-ethnic settings. You never seem to have a problem mixing with people of all colors, shapes, and backgrounds. And yet, when you're in a more homogeneous group, your whole demeanor changes.

I've heard you tell jokes that are mean, not funny. I've seen you characterize entire groups as being murderous, miserly, or thieving. I've listened to you talk, in the most derogatory terms, about people who are "guilty" only of being of different faiths.

Perhaps you're not aware of the impact your words have. Perhaps you're trying to appeal to the base nature of one or two people whose approval is important to you. Perhaps you're trying to downplay your education and intelligence, for whatever reason.

But on the off-chance that you're not aware of it, I, and others in our crowd, have come to think of you as a bigot. That's an ugly term, Lance, and I doubt you'd like it applied to you. I think you need to look in the mirror and decide who you are.

With concern,

Paul Baxter

• Giving the reader the "out" that they may not be aware of their behavior makes the letter less threatening.

• Take responsibility for your words. Say "I think," "I've heard," etc. Don't hide behind what others say.

Name
Address
City, State Zip

Date

Coach Armand Arroyo
Woodside High School
15 Palisade Avenue
Knoxville, TN 37914

Dear Coach Arroyo:

I encouraged my son Greg's participation in after-school team sports because I believed it would give him a sense of belonging and self-esteem. The plan has backfired.

Because of your coaching style, Greg is more withdrawn and unsure of himself than he was before he joined your team.

I've attended every game and watched my son sit on the bench. During the entire season, he has never been given an opportunity to play, and he tells me that you constantly humiliate him by calling him "super spazz."

This is enrichment? This is team spirit? You need to re-think your obligations as an educator and a coach. Kids need to learn less about competition and more about playing the game.

I'm sending a copy of this letter to the director of athletics and the superintendent of schools. Perhaps you can be persuaded by them, if not by me, to give each member of your team a shot at success.

Sincerely,

Sherry Palmer

- Express your grievance, and back it up with specific examples.

- Tell the reader how you would like their attitude or behavior to change.

I'm Gay, to Friend (15-19)

Name
Address
City, State Zip

Date

Dear Bonnie and Richard,

Someone once said to me that friends are people who know all about you and like you anyway. I hope I can count on you to live up to that definition.

Over the years, I convinced myself that I wasn't hiding anything by not telling you I was gay. After all, I reasoned, our friendship had nothing to do with my sexual orientation.

Times have changed, though. I now believe that I was deliberately hiding my homosexuality from you. I'm not sure why, since it's part of who I am, and I'm comfortable with myself and my life.

I've finally decided that keeping the truth from you has been causing me a great deal of discomfort. So now you know.

I hope this news won't change our relationship in any way. Your friendship and support mean so much to me. Please keep in touch.

Faithfully,

Miles

- Using an adage, like this one about friends, can set the tone for the entire letter.

- Giving people the impression that you expect them to take news well makes it more likely that they will.

Name
Address
City, State Zip

Date

Dear Elizabeth,

I dealt with my mother's death by withdrawing from people. I felt a need for complete privacy, and asked all my friends—including you—to respect my desire to be alone.

You're the only one who viewed my grieving process as a personal rejection. Even though you were the first person I called after my isolation, you were abrupt and almost confrontational.

I had the right to work my way through a devastating loss on my own terms. I'm disappointed that a month has passed since that conversation and you still haven't made any attempt to contact me.

We've known each other for a long time, Elizabeth, but you let me down when I really needed your understanding and support. I guess we didn't have much of a relationship, after all.

With many regrets,

Deborah

- If you've been severely disappointed by someone close to you, you may wish to tell them so, even if it means ending the relationship.

- Be sure to explain yourself so there can be no mistaking your message.

Name
Address
City, State Zip

Date

Dear Lizette,

You achieved a unique record. Virtually everyone at my dinner party had a comment to make about you.

The men seemed to enjoy your company. At different times, each one conveyed to me that he felt you were bright, witty and charming. The women were also of a unanimous opinion; they felt ignored by you. They claimed that every word you uttered was directed to the men, with no attempt made to include the women or even acknowledge them.

I'm not repeating any of this to make you feel uncomfortable. I just thought you should be aware of how you're being perceived. I feel badly that my women friends dismissed you; I was hoping you would become a part of our social group

If you'd like to talk about doing some repair work, give me a call.

Your friend,

Sheila

- People often "play to an audience," without being aware of the consequences of their actions.

- If you're willing to discuss the behavior, tell the person so. You may be preventing their being excluded from future events.

Name
Address
City, State Zip

Date

Dear Kent,

There's a school of thought that says an individual is only responsible for his own behavior...that he can only embarrass himself. I don't subscribe to that belief; I was totally embarrassed by your behavior.

I brought you to the meeting because you asked for an invitation; I didn't drag you there against your will. It was bad enough that you felt a need to smoke in a non-smoking room. But to get into a shouting match about the rights of smokers was unconscionable. You were my guest, and I expected you to act like one.

If you still have hopes of joining the organization, you'll have to start with a letter of apology to the entire group. And then you'll need to find a different sponsor. I won't put myself in that position again.

Sincerely,

Jeffrey

- There's no need to tip-toe around the issue.

- Briefly describe the behavior that embarrassed you.

Name
Address
City, State Zip

Date

Dear Claudia,

I'm sorry that you're angry with me, but your anger is based on misinformation. I told Erin that if you needed a ride to the dance you should call me, and I'd arrange one for you. I didn't say I'd pick you up.

I don't know if Erin misstated what I said, or if you misunderstood her. I would never have said I would pick you up because you live nearly an hour out of my way. There are at least three people—all within a few miles of your apartment—who would gladly have picked you up if they had known you needed a ride.

I feel badly that you waited for a ride that never came. The only thing I might have done differently was to deliver the message personally, instead of through a third party. Since this was a misunderstanding, can we put this incident behind us?

Please let me hear from you.

Your friend,

Betsy

• It's often easier to analyze what went wrong in writing, rather than verbally.

• If the reader's reaction was based on bad information, and you want to maintain the friendship, tell the reader there are no hard feelings.

Name
Address
City, State Zip

Date

Dear Dad Brown:

Ray and I work very hard to teach the kids respect for all beliefs, so it's disheartening to hear them parrot some of your comments about other people's religion.

They've told one neighborhood child that they didn't want his kind around any more, and threatened to beat him up. When I asked them where they got such ideas, the response was, "Grandpa Brown said..."

There are many different beliefs, and it's important that we treat others with kindness, and set a good example for the children.

From now on, will you please keep your thoughts about this subject to yourself.

I appreciate your understanding.

Fondly,

Dottie

- Anger usually causes more anger. A firm, but moderate, tone is less antagonistic and equally effective.

- State what you feel is unacceptable to eliminate confusion and misunderstanding.

You Didn't Show Up for the Party I Gave for You (15-25)

Name
Address
City, State Zip

Date

Dear Patti,

After knocking myself out to help you become established in this area, I asked myself a lot of questions this weekend:

Why wouldn't you show up at a party I arranged, at <u>your</u> request, to help you meet new people?

Why were you at a club less than a mile from my apartment, when you were supposed to be here? (A mutual acquaintance saw you there.)

Why would you put me in the awkward, embarrassing position of trying to explain to my friends why the guest of honor didn't show?

How could you let the weekend go without so much as a call or attempt at an explanation?

Suddenly, the answer to every question hit me: You're a jerk.

Completely disgusted,

Janet

• Using a series of related questions builds to a climax.

• If it's more important to get something off your chest than to create a dialogue, saying something shocking works wonders. Just think about the potential consequences before sending the letter.

Name
Address
City, State Zip

Date

Dear Kim,

I was hurt that I wasn't invited to your daughter's wedding. For months preceding the event, you spoke about it so much, I couldn't imagine not being there to celebrate with you. In fact, I told my husband to get ready for what I was sure would be a spectacular affair.

With only a few weeks remaining before the wedding, it finally occurred to me that an invitation would not be forthcoming. I was disappointed because we've worked together for so long, I thought we had a relationship beyond that of colleagues.

I'm happy for you and your family, and I'm truly glad to hear that the wedding was such a success. However, I'd appreciate it if you'd stop talking about the wedding in my presence, since it hurts me every time you mention it.

Sincerely,

Judy

- It's healthier to express your feelings, rather than have them build up.

- If you see the person who offended you on a regular basis (as with a coworker), it's a good idea to send a letter that expresses your feelings without alienating them.

You Didn't Act like a Friend (15-27)

Name
Address
City, State Zip

Date

Dear Ross,

Maybe I have unrealistic expectations. But I believe in the Golden Rule. I treat people the way I'd like them to treat me.

I've been a loyal friend to you. That's why I don't think it's unreasonable to expect loyalty in return.

Your failure to defend me against unfair accusations is a great disappointment to me. If this is the way you behave towards friends, I'll have to reevaluate our friendship.

I feel betrayed. Perhaps you can offer an explanation.

Sincerely,

Eileen

- Tell the reader how they disappointed you.
- Ask for an explanation.

Name
Address
City, State Zip

Date

Dear Dale,

I was flattered that you asked me to attend your company picnic.
It meant you thought enough of me to want to introduce me to
your friends and colleagues. At least that's what I originally
thought.

But as soon as we arrived, you jumped into a softball game that
lasted nearly two hours. I was alone on the sideline, not knowing
a soul, feeling very awkward about having to introduce myself to
strangers. And this pattern continued throughout the day. You'd
bring me something to eat or drink, then run off to talk with your
buddies.

How could you be so insensitive? Didn't you realize how I'd feel
among two hundred strangers? You invited me to spend the day
with you, but the only thing we shared that day was being in the
same zip code.

I'm disappointed in you, Dale. Your lack of sensitivity is a real
threat to our relationship.

Sincerely,

Joan

- Someone who is insensitive won't "get it" on their own. You need to spell out the offending behavior.

- By ending with a statement of disapproval (as opposed to termination), you're leaving enough room for the other person to respond.

Name
Address
City, State Zip

Date

Dear Theresa,

I know from personal experience how quickly "cabin fever" can overwhelm a young mother. That's why I agreed to babysit occasionally for Jennifer. I guess I should have defined "occasionally."

Last week Jennifer spent three afternoons at my house. And on two of those occasions you dropped her off without even calling first. Jennifer is a darling child and I enjoy spending time with her, but I feel I'm being taken advantage of. That's why I'm withdrawing my offer to babysit.

Sincerely,

Bess

- Explain how a change in the situation has affected your decision.

- Accept responsibility if part of the problem is your fault.

Name
Address
City, State Zip

Date

Dear Mark,

The invitation to your financial planning seminar came within days of my father's death, and it offended me. I would have preferred to receive a note of condolence before receiving an offer of advice on my inheritance.

Don't expect me at your seminar. At this time, financial planning is the farthest thing from my mind.

Sincerely,

Melissa Pasco

- Be clear about your reason for declining the invitation.

- If you are annoyed about someone's behavior, a succinct letter can sometimes say it better than you could in person.

Name
Address
City, State Zip

Date

Dear Bill,

In the past, when you asked me to contribute to charitable causes, I never hesitated. But this time I'm saying no.

A few months ago I saw an unfavorable news report about Helping Hands, and it stayed in my mind. The report showed convincing evidence that the administrators of Helping Hands are pocketing a high percentage of the contributions.

Unless I can be certain that my donations are going to be well spent, I don't write a check.

I'd be glad to consider any future requests for worthwhile causes.

Sincerely,

Ellen Scheel

- Explain your reason for not contributing.

- Put the onus on the reader to change your mind by providing additional information.

Name
Address
City, State Zip

Date

Dear Brett,

Your request for a letter of reference puts me in a awkward position. I require evidence of three qualities before I'll recommend someone for a job:

1) A willingness to work hard
2) A desire to learn
3) A positive attitude toward coworkers

You've shown that you can be a hard worker and you're receptive to new ideas, but I think you need to examine your attitude toward your colleagues—specifically, editors.

You may be great at researching articles, but without the contributions of the editors, even your best work wouldn't be polished enough to print. Yet on several occasions I've seen you treat the editors with disdain.

I regret not being able to write you a letter of reference. But I hope you'll benefit from my comments about your attitude.

Sincerely,

Kathleen Casey

• State your criteria for giving a reference.

• State how the reader doesn't meet the criteria.

Name
Address
City, State Zip

Date

Dear Marilyn,

Your recent request for a loan made me think of a quote by Shakespeare—not the cliched section about borrowing and lending, but the rest of the passage, which has personal meaning for me. It continues, "For loan oft loses both itself and friend."

My experience has been that hard feelings ensue when money is at stake. I don't want to lose your friendship, so I'm going to pass on the loan. It's a matter of principle, and I'm not comfortable making an exception.

I hope you understand.

Kindest regards,

Sue

- Explain your reason for not lending money.

- State firmly that you won't make an exception.

Name
Address
City, State Zip

Date

Dear Ellie,

It isn't easy saying no to a friend. Especially when the request seems so simple. But a recent experience has soured me on the idea of lending my clothes.

I lent an outfit to someone, and it was returned to me with permanent stains. I made a vow that I'd never lend my clothes again—to anyone!

I know how responsible you are, but I just can't risk damage to the dress—or worse—damage to our friendship.

Please understand.

Love,

Liz

- Explain why you won't lend the item.

- Tell the reader that your decision is based on past experience, not on a character judgement.

I Won't Lie for You (15-35)

Name
Address
City, State Zip

Date

Dear Peter,

I'm willing to assume responsibility for my own actions, but not for yours. I won't lie for you, and I resent your asking.

This is your problem. Please leave me out of it.

Sincerely,

Margo

- State your position firmly.

- It's O.K. to sound irate when someone has asked you to compromise your values.

Name
Address
City, State Zip

Date

Dear Alex,

I've run out of patience and I won't rescue you again. You need help for your addiction, and until you make an effort to get it, I'm withdrawing my support.

Reading about addiction has taught me three things:

1) I didn't cause your addiction.
2) I can't control your addiction.
3) I can't cure your addiction.

I'll help you find a recovery program. I'll drive you to meetings. But I won't support your habit.

I care very much about what happens to you. Now you have to care, too.

Fondly,

Karen

- Tell the reader what you *won't* do. Then tell them what you *will* do.

- Explain your motivation.

Sympathy and Condolences 16

When writing a letter of sympathy or condolence, don't claim the reader's grief or disappointment as your own. By carrying on endlessly about your *own* emotions, you defeat the purpose of the letter—which is to respectfully acknowledge the reader's misfortune. If you've experienced a similar loss, it can be helpful to share how you overcame your own ordeal, but keep the focus of your sympathy on the reader.

Sympathy. The sympathy letter is the antidote to the song, "Nobody Knows You When You're Down and Out." It's an expression of support, designed to help the reader through a tough time. Let your letter convey a sense of caring and concern. State your desire to help in a specific way (i.e., providing transportation, lodging, helping with meals, babysitting, etc.). Finally, express a positive outlook.

Condolences. Many people quake at the thought of writing a condolence letter, out of fear of saying the wrong thing. It's true that words of condolence should be carefully chosen, but the extra effort will be appreciated by the reader. Convey your shock or sadness upon hearing the news. Convey a sense of sympathy about the reader's loss. Share a meaningful recollection about the person who has passed away. Offer to help in any way you can.

The approach you take with your condolence letter will vary according to the circumstances. The death of an elderly person after a lengthy illness would be acknowledged differently from the sudden death of a healthy person. The death of a child would be acknowledged differently from the death of an adult. Similarly, the reader's relationship to the deceased will influence the overall tone of your letter.

A condolence letter can't reverse tragic or unfortunate events. It *can* offer comfort and support.

Name
Address
City, State Zip

Date

Dear Mike,

I thought of you this morning as I was thumbing through an old Sports Illustrated article. Wayne Gretzky (your idol, as I recall) was quoted as saying, "I skate to where the puck is going to be, not to where it has been." Does that make sense to you? Gretzky was saying that if you don't look ahead, you fall behind.

You're my favorite nephew, Mike, and I don't like seeing you concentrate on what didn't happen, rather than on what did. You're putting all your energy into not having been accepted at an Ivy League school, instead of preparing for the wonderful experience that you'll have at Strathmore.

I'll see you during Christmas break...and I can't wait to hear about your first taste of college life. Congratulations on your acceptance to Strathmore; it's a great school!

Love,

Uncle Rich

- A quote from a celebrity is often helpful in making a point.

- Congratulate the reader on positive achievements.

Name
Address
City, State Zip

Date

Dear Shelly,

It's understandable that you'd feel disappointed you didn't pass the bar exam on your first try. That's only natural after all the effort you put into preparing for it.

But when we spoke, you sounded as if you were ready to throw in the towel. From what I hear, many successful attorneys need two or more attempts to make it.

When I was younger and thought I had hit bottom (more than once), your grandfather would sit me down and say, "The fight's not over 'til you're down for the count."

In other words, you've only begun to fight. You've got everything it takes to make a great lawyer. But you'll never make it unless you believe that. I do.

Love,

Dad

- Don't minimize the disappointment, but remind the reader that it's only a temporary setback.

- Reaffirm your faith in the individual's abilities.

Name
Address
City, State Zip

Date

Dear Vic,

Alfred Fuller, the man who started the Fuller Brush Company, was fired from his first three jobs. The fellow I currently work for admits to being fired twice prior to building his own business. (His wife once told me he was "modest" about his past; that he had actually been fired an amazing five times!)

The point, of course, is that you're too good to let this one bad experience get you down. You sounded awful on the phone, and right now you don't have the luxury of feeling sorry for yourself. You have to get your resume out, hit the road for some interviews, and get your confidence level back up.

Why don't you send me a copy of your resume and I'll see what I can do to help update it. I'll also tell the guys at work to keep their eyes and ears open.

I'll talk to you soon. Keep your chin up.

Your friend,

Charlie

P.S. If it makes you feel any better, Lee Iacocca was fired by Ford, Ronald Reagan by Warner Brothers, etc., etc.

• It's helpful to put a firing in perspective. The message is that others have been fired and rebounded from it.

• If you're going to offer help, be sure that you'll deliver on it.

Name
Address
City, State Zip

Date

Dear Rick,

On the one hand, I'm sorry to hear that you were caught in a surprise layoff. The consensus is that your company overreacted to a down business cycle. Chances seem good, based on what I've been reading in the paper, that there may be a callback very soon.

On the other hand, you might choose to think of this "break" as giving you an opportunity to look at other employment possibilities. For example, I've wanted you to apply for a job at my company for a long time, and now you have the incentive to do so.

In fact, there are a number of companies you ought to check out while you have the time to interview. I'd be happy to give you some suggestions.

You're too talented to be out for long, Rick. Just make the most of your time off. Keep thinking of Thomas Edison's credo, "Everything comes to him who hustles while he waits."

Best,

Jason

- Encourage the reader to seek other employment unless rehiring is guaranteed.

- Bolster the reader's sense of self-worth.

Name
Address
City, State Zip

Date

Dear Jeb,

It's frustrating to be put on "hold" when you're making a phone call. It must be <u>awful</u> to have to put your whole life on hold because of an accident.

I'm sorry that you've been sidelined by the car crash. I hope your discomfort is minimal and that your broken leg heals quickly.

I'd feel that I was contributing to your recuperation if you'd let me feed your fish, water your plants or pick up some groceries for you. Just say the word. (P.S.—I don't do windows.)

In the meantime, get well. And call if you need HELP!

Fondly,

Cara

- Try to lift the reader's spirits with a mixture of humor and compassion.

- Offer to help out in any way you can (e.g., run errands, make phone calls, take care of pets, etc.).

Name
Address
City, State Zip

Date

Dear Carrie,

I know you're experiencing a difficult transition, and I'd like to offer you a sympathetic ear.

Facing life as a single person, after years of togetherness, is a scary prospect. The motto that's been most helpful to me is "one day at a time." If that doesn't work, try "one <u>hour</u> at a time!"

We're rarely prepared for change, but frequently it can be a blessing. At the very least it's an opportunity for growth.

I'm confident that you'll emerge from this passage with a new sense of yourself. I did.

Fondly,

Veronica

- Offer the reader your support and compassion.

- Share your own experience (or one you're familiar with) as proof that a positive transition is possible.

Name
Address
City, State Zip

Date

Dear Marcy and Donald,

We've said a prayer of thanks that your family escaped the fire unharmed, but my heart goes out to you at the destruction of your home.

We can't fathom the emotional toll of such a loss, but we hope you'll let us help in any way we can.

Please accept our offer of food, clothing, transportation, or a place to stay. You've just got to get the family out of that motel.

We'll call in a couple of days, after you've had time to decide how we can be of greatest assistance.

Affectionately,

Sandy and Bill Demarest

- Express your sympathy.

- Offer the kind of assistance that you can follow up on.

Name
Address
City, State Zip

Date

Dear Maddie,

What a terrible disappointment you've had. You and Bob were so excited about becoming parents. It must be extremely painful to deal with the loss.

I hope the support of your family and friends will ease your sadness. Please let me know what I can do to help.

Love,

Roberta

- Acknowledge what a difficult time this is for the reader.

- Remind the reader that family and friends can be helpful in overcoming the grief.

Name
Address
City, State Zip

Date

Dear Cal,

One of the things I admire about you is your ability to juggle ten projects at once and make it look effortless. Knowing the stress that you're experiencing in your personal life makes your unflappable demeanor even more impressive.

I'm sorry that Ruth is not well. It must be a real challenge for you to shoulder the responsibilities of home and work simultaneously.

Your wife's health is your top priority, and it's important that you spend time with her. If there's anything I can do to lessen your load at work, please tell me.

As your friend and colleague, I offer my support and my sincere wishes for Ruth's full recovery.

Cordially,

Polly

- Acknowledge the reader's stressful situation.

- Offer to help out in any way that's feasible.

Name
Address
City, State Zip

Date

Dear Art,

My instinct is to say, "I hope you're feeling better after your operation!"

My experience tells me, however, that most people feel <u>worse</u> after an operation—at least temporarily. May you be the exception!

But you can't keep a good man down. That's why I know you'll recover in record time.

Get well soon.

Fondly,

Alice

- You don't need to get specific about the nature of the surgery. The point is to let the reader know you're thinking of them.

- Keep the tone of the letter optimistic and light.

Name
Address
City, State Zip

Date

Dear Hildy,

The office is positively dismal without you. We miss your energy and creative stimulation. That's why I'm insisting that you get well ASAP!

If I can tie up any loose business for you, just give a yell. But don't expect me to inspire the troops—that's what we've got you for!

Kindest regards,

Marcus

• Reassure the reader of their value to the company.

• Try to make them feel an ongoing connection to the workplace.

Name
Address
City, State Zip

Date

Dear Aunt Edith,

I was sorry to hear that you've had to endure another bout of phlebitis. But I was happy to learn that you're recovering well. Uncle Jim tells me that you're following the doctor's orders and staying relatively immobile.

You know how much my kids love you, don't you? Well, I promised them a trip to see you next month, assuming you're feeling better. Kathy said she's not sure if that's such a great incentive for you to get well fast! The children can be a bit rambunctious.

We'll keep tabs on you. And assuming you're up to a visit, we'll set a date with you in a few weeks. Be sure you listen to the doctor and Uncle Jim.

I love you. Hope to see you soon.

Your nephew,

Will

• When someone is ill and vulnerable, it's important for family to acknowledge the illness and offer support.

• Many people do not like drop-in visits when they're ill. It's best to say you'd like to see the individual, and to make sure they want to see you, too.

Get Well, to Friend (16-13)

Name
Address
City, State Zip

Date

Dear Bud,

We decided to hold our regular Friday night poker game, even though you couldn't be there. The other guys might not admit it to you, but I will: It wasn't the same without you.

You know how much Ron gripes about your cigars? Would you believe he said he missed the "aroma"? Arnie complained that you're the only one who ever tells decent jokes, and that he was bored with the rest of us. And Dave said that he missed having a patsy to take advantage of.

The point is, we all miss you and hope your knee's on the mend. (I haven't been very conscientious about my morning jog without you to push me.) As to the card game, as soon as you can get around on crutches, we expect you back. I hope the doctors left a few dollars for us!

Get well soon!

Best wishes,

Ben

• People love to know they're missed. Make it a point to say so to a friend who's layed up.

• Personal quotes from acquaintances help the sick party feel less isolated.

Name
Address
City, State Zip

Date

Dear Marilyn and Jon,

I'm so sad that Eddie's brave battle with cancer was unsuccessful. Your loss is more than any family should have to bear.

You gave your son the best: medically, emotionally and spiritually. He had splendid parents during his short time on earth; of that I'm certain.

Eddie taught me more about courage than any ten grown-ups. It's a lesson I'll never forget. Just as I'll never forget Jonathan Edward Bascomb, Jr.

My thoughts and prayers are with you.

With love,

Miranda

• Express your conviction that the reader gave their best to the child.

• Communicate a personal memory of the child or your view of the legacy they left behind.

Name
Address
City, State Zip

Date

Dear Phil,

Whenever I think of Tony, I think of you. You were such close pals that you used to finish each other's sentences. That's why I understand how empty you must feel without him.

I hope you realize how much he admired and respected you. He often told me that your encouragement provided the incentive he needed to turn his life around. He was very grateful, and he let everybody know it.

If you need someone to talk to, I hope you'll call me. I'm no substitute for Tony, but I'd be happy to fill in the gaps any way I can.

Sincerely,

Micky

• Acknowledge the reader's close relationship with the deceased.

• Share a positive memory or anecdote.

Name
Address
City, State Zip

Date

Dear Rosemarie,

I'm so sorry that Walt has lost his struggle. You both fought so hard. Your fortitude in the face of Walt's illness has been remarkable.

I believe you found your strength in the relationship that you and Walt shared. You'll always have memories of the wonderful years you spent together.

Please let me know how I can help you through this lonely time.

Fondly,

Cora

• Express your admiration for the reader's courage.

• Inject a positive note about the future, and offer any help you can.

Name
Address
City, State Zip

Date

Dear Bob,

The news of Hannah's sudden death has shaken me. I feel angry that Fate has delivered such a cruel blow to you and your family.

Hannah was a vibrant person: at home, at work, and in the community. She brought out the best in people by setting high standards for herself. It's inconceivable that she's gone.

I'm placing myself at your disposal. If you need a babysitter, a cook, an errand-runner or a sympathetic ear—please call me. I hope you'll allow me to help you get through this.

With deepest sympathy,

Deborah

- Acknowledge the shock that is caused by a sudden death.

- Convey the sense of loss that you share with the reader.

Name
Address
City, State Zip

Date

Dear Florence,

This past year has been a really trying time for you.

I've admired your dedication to your mother during her illness.
She couldn't have asked for a more devoted daughter.

Just as you brought comfort to your mother, I hope that her
memory will bring comfort to you. She was a courageous,
energetic woman with a wonderful sense of humor.

I see the same traits in you. What a legacy she has left!

With love,

Grace

• Acknowledge the stress of a long illness.

• Offer an uplifting thought about the lasting connection between parent and child.

Name
Address
City, State Zip

Date

Dear Lauren,

It's much too soon to have to write this letter. You and your Mom should have had many more years together. She was supposed to see her grandchildren grow up.

Even those of us who were not related to her felt her love and caring. I already feel her absence.

If you feel like talking, please pick up the phone. I know you and your Mom enjoyed late night gabfests. I'm an especially good listener in those hours between midnight and dawn.

My thoughts and prayers are with you.

With love,

Maggie

- It's all right to express a sense of anger and disbelief.

- Offer to make yourself available to the reader as they go through the grieving process.

Name
Address
City, State Zip

Date

Dear Tara,

There isn't any way to prepare for the loss of a parent. I remember feeling so vulnerable when my Dad died—suddenly, the loving parent I had always turned to was gone. I felt as though I had to act grown up, but I felt very child-like.

You have my sympathy as you make your way through this passage. It won't be easy, but you can rely on the support of all your friends.

I didn't know your father, but he must have been quite a guy. Just look at his daughter.

Fond regards,

Evelyn

- If you can, share the wisdom you've gleaned from losing a loved one.

- Convey the thought that the parent lives on in the child.

Name
Address
City, State Zip

Date

Patricia Covington, Ph.D.
1902 Westmoreland Road
Chestnut Hill, MA 02167

Dear Pat:

This note may be late in coming (I just found out about Ralph's death), but the message is heartfelt.

Reading about Ralph made me appreciate how much he contributed during his life and why you always spoke so admiringly of him. I feel especially saddened that I never had the opportunity to meet him. What a unique person he must have been.

With deepest sympathy,

Samuel Wheeler

• It's better to be late than not to respond.

• If you haven't met the deceased, don't talk about them as if you did; it will make you seem insincere.

Name
Address
City, State Zip

Date

Dear Mary Ellen and Wayne,

We were sorry to learn that Thor passed away. He was such a great and loyal companion. It's hard to believe that he won't come racing out to greet us the next time we visit.

We understand your sense of loss. We still miss Corky, even though he's been gone for six years.

With sympathy,

Nancy and Dennis

• Treat the loss of a pet as you would any other loss. (This is hard for non-pet owners to understand, but valid nonetheless.)

• An example of how the pet will be missed personalizes your message.

Response to Condolence Letter (16-23)

Name
Address
City, State Zip

Date

Dear Veronica and Paul,

We so much appreciated your note; it was filled with such kindness and love. We need all the support we can get right now.
Our hearts ache.

Patrick was a son who shared all his joy with us. He was so
happily married—for two short years—and was such a doting
father to eight-month-old Erica. We're hoping Patrick's wife and
the baby will spend some time with us this summer.

Thank you for your thoughtfulness.

With affection,

Claire and Michael

• When someone cares enough about you to express sympathy, it's equally thoughtful to respond with a thank you.

• Since people are interested, you may wish to share some information on how the family is coping.

Index by Title

Index by Subject

(**Boldface** numbers indicate chapter introductions. Numbers in parentheses are document numbers found at the top of each letter. They are followed by page numbers.)

A

Accountants, letters to, **274**
  about high bill (12-15), 289
  about missing deduction (12-14), 288
Angry letters (*See* Complaints; Getting it off your chest; Hurt feelings; Saying no; Telling it like it is)
Anniversary (*See* Congratulations; Invitations)
Apologies, **1-2**
  about event
    for being out of town for your award (1-04), 6
    for being unable to come to party (1-08), 10
    for breaking CD player (1-05), 7
    for burning hole in sofa (1-06), 8
    for drinking too much (1-07), 9
    for forgetting our anniversary (1-11), 13

    for forgetting your birthday (1-09), 11
    for forgetting your birthday, poem (1-10), 12
    for my child misbehaving (1-01), 3
    for my pet causing trouble (1-02), 4
    for spoiling your party (1-03), 5
  about feelings
    for being inconsiderate (1-18), 20
    for betraying confidence (1-13), 15
    for blaming you (1-12), 14
    for hurting your feelings (1-14), 16
    for lying to you (1-15), 17
    for misleading you (1-16), 18
    for the misunderstanding (1-17), 19
    for slighting you (1-20), 22
    for starting a fight (1-19), 21

B

Bad news, **93-94** (*See also* Telling it like it is)
  about illness and death
    Dad is having operation (4-15), 109

you didn't understand my needs
(15-20), 402
you embarrassed me (15-22), 404
you had the facts wrong (15-23), 405
you ignored me (15-28), 410
you set a bad example for my
children (15-24), 406

I

J

request to serve as honorary
chairperson (14-10), 350
civic
come to neighborhood meeting
(14-12), 352
join organization (14-13), 353
resignation from organization
(14-15), 355
would you speak at meeting
(14-14), 354

P

Parents, letters to (*See* Holiday
correspondence; Letters
home, to parents;
Thank you's)
Party (*See* Invitations; Thank you's)
Poems, **65** (*See* Apologies; Congratulations)
Praise, **291** (*See also* Thank you's)
to athletic coach (7-15), 197
to company president (7-12), 194
to congressperson (7-10), 192
to President (7-09), 191
to tutor (13-07), 299
you improved your school grades
(13-04), 296
you led the team to victory (13-05),
297
you made me proud (13-01), 293
you responded well in crisis (13-06),
298
you showed courage (13-03), 295
you showed patriotism (13-02), 294
Professionals (*See* Accountants, letters
to; Doctors, letters to;
Lawyers, letters to)

Public officials, letters to (*See* Getting
it off your chest)

R

References, **215-216**
for former employee (9-07), 223
request to employer, for work
(9-06), 222
request to friend, for country club
(9-08), 224
request to teacher, for college (9-05),
221
Reminders, **94**
pay your share of phone bill (4-29),
123
remove furniture from our basement
(4-31), 125
repay money (4-28), 122
return dress (4-27), 121
your turn to take care of Grandma
(4-30), 124
Requests for assistance and information
(*See* Education; Government,
letters to; Organizations;
Senior citizens; Travel)
Resignations, **161-162**
to be full-time mom (6-15), 177
due to illness (6-13), 175
I'm moving (6-16), 178
I'm retiring (6-17), 179
spouse being transferred (6-14), 176
Responses to requests (*See* Saying no)

S

Saying no, **381-382**
won't babysit anymore (15-29), 411
won't give to charity (15-31), 413

to organizations
    for contribution (13-42), 334
    for creating apprenticeship
        program (13-44), 336
    for grant (13-43), 335
    for providing speaker (13-46),
        338
    for sponsoring team (13-45), 337
Travel, **340**
    reservation
        cancellation of (14-37), 377
        confirmation of (14-36), 376

requests
    for confirmation of travel costs
        (14-34), 374
    for estimate of travel costs
        (14-33), 373
    for information about health
        issues (14-39), 379
    for passport application (14-38),
        378
    for travel information (14-35),
        375